BECAUSE I'M SUITABLE

THE JOURNEY OF A WIFE ON DUTY (REVISED)

ALLISON P. URIBE

WIVES ON DUTY
—— MINISTRIES ——
SUPPORT· ENCOURAGE· INSPIRE

Cover Design: Adam Davis

Typesetting: Adam Davis

The Lord God said, "It is not good for the man to be alone. I will make a helper suitable for him."
Genesis 2:18 NLT

This book is dedicated to my parents
Mr. and Mrs.
Mario and Rosie Perez

For the all late night dances I secretly saw in a dark living room. For showing me what perseverance looks like in love. For all the wisdom you have poured into my marriage with and without words. But, most of all, for teaching me that nothing is impossible with God. God couldn't have blessed me with more perfect parents. I love you both so much.

CONTENTS

Introduction   ix

I Do   1
From Miss to Mrs   11
I Now Pronounce You Husband and Wife   21
Love Is Patient, Love Is Kind   33
A Good Thing   47
The Real Enemy   63
A Story For Impact   87
Our Heavenly Substation   101
And On The Seventh Day   133
The Pursuit   147

Afterword   157
The Staining of the Bride   161
About the Author   165

INTRODUCTION

A suitable helper. What does that mean? Could it be that the life of a first responder wife was all a part of God's original plan? For when God saw man alone and knew it was not good, he sent a suitable helper to complete a creative masterpiece. This masterpiece known as marriage, was created to reflect the church. Some men and women have chosen to stand by first responders in marriage. Who does God send? A suitable helper. The word "suitable" should echo in our heart and thoughts so fiercely.

SUITABLE: (Adj)- right or appropriate for a particular person, purpose, or situation.

This definition reveals that God sees you as right for the man you are married to. It allows us to see that we are fitting as a wife and no matter the situation or circumstances, God sees you as suitable. This should open our eyes to see that God has a purpose and plan for marriage, including first responder marriages. We are two imperfect people who love imperfectly. God being the grace we need, comes in when invited, loving perfectly through us. When God is invited into our marriage and life, He takes us, our purpose, and situations into His hands. It is then God helps us in our actions, words, and decisions to be suitable. We are suitable for not only our first responder and ourselves, but for the very purpose we hold in our life.

I remember driving one afternoon thanking God for restoring my marriage. I sat at a stoplight when I could hear Him say, "You are suitable. I saw the struggles, but you forgot that you were suitable. I created you with so much purpose and being Joe's wife is one of them. I can express my love to him through you, and it is my will that I express my love to you through him. But always know I saw you as Joe's suitable helper and so much more. You are enough."

Marriage to a first responder may hold challenges, I know our marriage faced many. This book is designed to challenge you as the wife of a first responder. Each chapter will contain experiences, questions, scriptures, and prayers. I encourage you as a first responder wife to always seek God first and foremost. It is important to also reach out if help is needed. If the situation in your marriage is unsafe or abusive in nature, please remove yourself and seek safety or shelter. But as you read through, remember you are more than enough. Although each of us may fail, just remember we are all a work in progress. It is a hope that our marriage testimony will encourage you in your wife on duty journey.

I DO

On November 23, 2001, I prepared to walk down the aisle in front of our wedding guests, and of course, God. I remember taking the deepest breath as I wrapped my arm around my father's. It was the exclusive walk moment, as I was to be escorted to the one my heart loved. As my father and I proceeded down the aisle, I couldn't help but smile. Everyone had their eyes on me and their genuine smiles encouraged me.

It was encouraging in the sense that they knew of our happiness, and I knew that their highest hopes would always be with us. Still, I wondered. How many people in the room were mentally betting on whether or not we would last? It may sound distasteful, but true. How many people attend

weddings, including yourself, often wonder about
the longevity of the marriage? Many times statistics
have already concluded their answer according to
your circumstances.

The walk down the aisle, for many, is the most heart
pounding, exciting anticipation a woman can ever
experience. It's the moment many girls dream
about. They imagine the fine foods, linens, décor,
the dress, and the Prince-Charming of a groom. A
wedding is such an extravagant affair filled with all
this investment. The bride and groom along with
their family give of their time, money, efforts, and
support. It turns into the event of the year without
the realization of what is truly taking place. A
promise, a vow, an oath is being declared before God
and others. Flowers, cathedral like buildings, the
glamour of décor can be all around the bride and
groom, but if there is no commitment behind their
vows, it was all for nothing.

As a chaplain, I have officiated numerous weddings.
I purposefully seek to speak alone with both the
bride and groom. I remind them that while their
venue is breathtaking, they must realize their vows
are the most important. I mention the importance of
their "vow moment" and how it is never to be
forgotten. They must always remember the love
they share which led them to the altar that day. If
only someone had mentioned the importance of
vows to me, perhaps I would have not gone through

the wedding day motions. You know, where the goal is just to get married, eat a fancy dinner, dance, and off to the honeymoon!

Well, I finally made it into his arms. It was my husband-to-be, me, and God. We stood there listening to the scriptures specifically relating to marriage. I remember focusing more on my groom as we smiled at each other completely lost in love and in the moment. The sermon was shared, scriptures were read, and finally the moment we longed for arrived. It was time to say our vows; time to say, "I do".

> *"That is why a man leaves his father and mother and is united to his wife, and they become one flesh"*
>
> — GENESIS 2:24 NIV

We faced each other and vowed before God to love one another, honor each other, care for one another in sickness and health, for better or worse, till death do us part. Wow! Those are some heavy duty promises! But I meant it, every word. I loved the man I was staring at in front of me. I loved the man behind him even more - the man on the cross. At the moment, I never knew our marriage would lead me into an immense understanding of God and his plan for both of us. I promised and vowed before the

Lord, in the church, not realizing its importance. After all, words are easier said than done. Perhaps a wedding in the church is expected by so many, but both of us were unaware of the true meaning behind it.

Marriage requires a lot of action by both husband and wife. I had not realized I would have to commit and perform out my vows, and my husband too. Love at that time was an incredible emotion to us both, yet we didn't comprehend it was purely action based. Of course, on our wedding day, we are joyful, and it's the most exciting day of our life. I think in those moments we would almost say anything just to get what we want – our spouse! However, what happens when things go wrong? In those troubling times will the words, "I do", mean anything? The words "I do" on our wedding day then take on a completely different significance, especially when it comes to trials in marriage. We must consistently ask ourselves if we can commit to such vows. Our vows are not an option, but a decision to be made each and every day.

For example, let's take a look at the oath our officers pledge. They are very similar! Receiving a badge requires dedication, and just like vows, an oath is expressed publicly. The oath taken then requires action from the one taking it on and making it their own. "To protect and serve" is the most popular declaration known in the law enforcement community. With all the chaos in this world, no matter the crisis at the assigned call, our officers are expected to protect and serve the citizens. There is no going back on their oath! According to The International Association of Chiefs of Police, the most widely spread oath spoken is this.....

"On my honor, I will never betray my badge, my integrity, my character or the public trust. I will always have the courage to hold myself and others accountable for our actions."

As you can see, vows and oaths taken require honor. They also require integrity, character, trust, accountability, and courage. What makes marriage any different? Even more so, in a law enforcement marriage. Why has society taken marital vows or oaths of honor as something conditional? Police work and marriage cannot be done without one main factor, and that is love. We have heard it in the scriptures,

"There is no greater love than this - that a man should lay down his life for his friends."

— JOHN 15:13 NLT

The world may never see bullets flying with an officer running in to shield the innocent. That's just it, what drives someone to leave their family in order to fulfill an oath to protect and serve? What drives a human being willing to lay down their life for another? This is a law enforcement marriage reality – the uncertainty of a safe return and so much more. Now, let's get back to the wedding day, shall we?

So there we were, joined together becoming a Mr. and Mrs. I was excited, scared, unsure, yet so certain all in one night. This was it; I was now married, and he and I were one flesh.

Of course I didn't expect everything to be perfect, but I figured if times got tough, we could handle it. I was a new bride with lots of new roads to journey on. There was so much more to be revealed about who we were, not only as individuals, but as a couple. I said, "I do" to a police officer. It was then I realized my marriage was in a class of its own. Of course, this was not a bad thing; this was the biggest blessing of my life. However, I had not understood the blessing it was.

Remember the wedding guests wondering about the longevity of our marriage? It is said that law enforcement marriages have a high divorce rate. I recall a friend telling me she didn't believe we would last two years. The cause? I am sure there are many factors. If you top the trauma from this line of work along with past life experiences, any marriage is bound to face trials. The truth is, as we walk down the aisle we are not alone. Our past hurts, pain, experiences, beliefs, or traditions follow us and become a part of who we are as a spouse. These past experiences affect our responses, emotions, and commitment. The calls our officers respond to on the beat play a huge role in how they respond to a variety of situations or stress. Equally, as the wife of an officer, walking the thin blue line beside them will also affect how you respond to situations. This can cause added stress as well.

Marriage is a gift not for the selfish, but for the unselfish. Marriage requires giving and sacrifice. Yet, how can we not walk into marriage with our minds set on our engrained beliefs? We were each raised in a certain way, so therefore we almost expect those ways to remain. However, marriage is where transformation begins. It will require one becoming who they need to be for the other. This is difficult for many to realize, but once it is, marriage can be a true adventure and healthy learning ground. Just as we are expected to grow as individuals, it does not exempt us from growing as a couple. If anything, marriage is its own growth opportunity. Through the years, one will find that the very past beliefs or pains they experienced, can become a strength. Arriving in such a place of strength will require the other spouse to be compassionate and sensitive. In that, it can aid the other in finding a healing place, not just within themselves, but within the marriage. Such a love starts from the beginning of a relationship and can only build from there. After all, marriage is all about building, and if built well, it will be made to last!

REFLECTION

- Looking back on your wedding day, what were your thoughts of the vows you made?
- At the time, did you say your vows to your husband alone, or did you vow to your husband and God?
- What were your hopes and dreams for your marriage as you walked down the aisle?
- To what do you feel God has called you in the role of an officer's wife?
- What is your prayer as you reflect on your wedding day?

Father,

As I reflect on our wedding day, I pray you will help me understand all I vowed before you. Reveal anything in my heart, in my actions, and in my speech that is displeasing to you in my role as a wife. Forgive me if I do not include you in our marital struggles. Show me how to be the wife on duty you called me to be. Show me how to turn to you alone and not to other temporary satisfactions. I pray that as I reflect, the love I have for my husband will grow deeper. I pray my heart embraces this beautiful role you have called me to as his helper. Lead my husband in the way he should go and give him the desire to fulfill his vows to me and oath to his city. As a couple help us to fulfill our commitment to one another, persevering through it all. Let me always remember I married a man, not an officer. Let us never lose focus of our dedication to one another. Give us the strength we need to walk the thin blue line.

In Jesus name,

Amen

TRUTH

For I know the plans I have for you,"
declares the Lord, "plans to prosper you
and not to harm you, plans to give you
hope and a future.

— JEREMIAH 29:11 NIV

Your eyes saw my unformed body; all the
days ordained for me were written in
your book before one of them came to be.

— PSALM 139:16 NIV

*In their hearts humans plan their course, but
the Lord establishes their steps.*

— PROVERBS 16:9 NIV

*He who finds a wife finds what is good and
receives favor from the LORD.*

— PROVERBS 18:22 NIV

*Two are better than one, because they have a
good return for their labor: If either of
them falls down, one can help the other
up. But pity anyone who falls and has no
one to help them up. Also, if two lie
down together, they will keep warm. But
how can one keep warm alone? Though
one may be overpowered, two can defend
themselves. A cord of three strands is not
quickly broken.*

— ECCLESIASTES 4:9-12 NIV

FROM MISS TO MRS

When we first met and began dating, my husband was new to the police force. He was fresh out of the academy and on duty throughout our first year together. He would share many experiences he had while on patrol. As a girlfriend, I listened with such interest and without interruption. It was all new to us as he discovered who he was as "Officer Uribe". I could sit and listen to all his bizarre and heroic stories as we ate dinner or walked hand in hand. It was like listening to a man on such an adventure I wanted so badly to be a part of. But soon that adventure became more realistic. He lost a brother in blue and it would be the first time I took part in this life, one who stood next to her first responder at a funeral.

As we walked toward the church that day, many
wives were walking with their officer, some standing
together in such somber unity. I took notice of the
wedding bands or the shiny badge necklace they
wore with such pride. Witnessing that brought a
longing to my heart. It was my deepest hope that
one day I would be the one he put a ring on. I
remember feeling like my role was not important. I
was a miss and not a Mrs. I guess you could say I
almost felt like I wasn't "in". I recall watching him
salute, watching him fight back tears, and admiring
his strength as he walked so sharply in uniform. I
often wonder if the pride I felt that day blinded me
from the call to duty and all it entailed.

As time passed in our dating journey, I found myself
screaming "yes" as I saw my officer on his knees
asking me to be his wife! It was not only the day of
my birthday, but the day I realized I was one step
closer to my heart's desire. Once again, it was all
adventure! But just like before, one night reality hit
too close to home. My phone rang one evening and
when I answered he said, "Babe, don't get worried,
but..." I am not sure what happened during the
conversation, but I remember starting to cry.

He had been injured on a foot chase and in that
moment I had not realized what worry, concern, and
burden I carried for his safety. Each night in our
dating relationship I was away from him, so when

we saw each other, our time together was precious. His injury would put him off the streets. He would need to prepare for surgery right before our wedding. The doctors mentioned there was a possibility he would be in a wheel chair on our wedding day.

Yet, all along, I just wanted to be his. Time passed after his eye-opening phone call and our wedding was being discussed. There were questions about his injury and decisions needing to be made in regards to the wedding and his recovery. During this time I remember my mom asked me, "Do you think you can be married to a police officer?" Tears welled up in my eyes and I remember it like it was yesterday, I said, "I don't know, but I know I love him." By the way, he was able to walk on our wedding day.

I realized the love for my officer was important, just as much as I was important in the role I had in his life. I couldn't allow my feelings of not being "in" affect me. The realization of the fact that I was "in" became more evident as time passed. This first responder life is a rough road to walk, but it can be done. God willing you are asked to be his Mrs., his bride, the one who gets his last name, you will still be able to do it. What really keeps all of us taking each day and step with our officer, is the love we have for them.

We never fell in love with the job, we fell in love with him, with whom he is, and who he would grow to be. The truth is our "I do" moment began with a proposal. All our relationship experiences prepare us for the walk down the aisle. When we are asked for our hand in marriage we respond with a "yes", an answer that says we are willing to do all possible to share a life together. As you can imagine, this only intensifies the walk down the aisle. It brings to light what a vow is to be. A wedding confirms an effective promise. An effective promise means that the vows we make will only transpire in the effectiveness of our love. Marriage changes things and transforms us. We become not who we want to be, but who we need to be for the sake of the other.

Being pronounced husband and wife is the beginning of a new journey. This journey will unpack many treasures that can only be found in time. Personally, as a "miss" I saw the surface, and as a "Mrs.", I saw the depth. Even in the greatest depth there is darkness, but there is also light to be found. Once I became a wife, I would come to know that learning all about him would take a life time.

There would be many attitudes, emotions, reactions, and seasons the two of us would experience. While we dreamt of our happily ever after, the reality of marriage was right before us. Perfection doesn't exist, we would both fail each other. But when we did fail, would we move forward unmoved or would we allow those failures to accumulate? Could this accumulation of failure to one another lead us apart? We could only hope not.

My father shared some wisdom with both my officer and I that I want to share with you. He said, "Even after you get married, never stop dating." Remember, marriage changes things, even how you view your spouse. Daily routines, children, work related stress, and time take away from you. I have heard time and time again how there is no time in the schedule for a date night. You must make time and protect that time. Intimacy is not only for the bedroom, but can be found in the deepest of conversations.

Date night can be a time to "check in" and make sure the both of you are in agreement. Be sure to hold hands, flirt, and some spontaneity never hurt anyone. I remember telling my officer how I missed when we would pick up pizza and watch a movie together in our dating days. One night after I put our children to sleep, I got into bed with the remote control and my officer came in the room with a hot pizza! We both laughed and enjoyed a movie together. Perhaps leaving the house is difficult for some of you, but there is always time for date night no matter where you are.

A police officer's call to duty has evolved along with their marriages. Whether you are dating or married to an officer, each one holds such weight. When I served as a chaplain with the police department, many officers would approach me seeking support for their girlfriend, fiancé, or wife. The concern in their eyes was precious to see. They too worry about their significant other being okay and feeling supported. As you can see, this call goes both ways for the officer and the one who stands beside them.

There is such a dying of self when you become involved in this life because of one thing, sacrifice. But really, isn't love sacrificial? Loving a first responder is not for the faint of heart, it is for those who maintain strength through the journey. The brave never truly journey alone, there is always love and a driving force behind them. No matter what season you are in with your officer, there is an effective promise unfolding.

Reflection

- Although we are wives, we must remember we were his girlfriend first. How does this change your perspective on being his Mrs.?
- Think back to your dating days, would you say your communication was greater back then or has it improved? If it hasn't

improved, what can you do to bring improvement?

- What comes to mind when you hear the word "sacrifice"?
- Was there ever reservation in your heart before you said "I do"? If so, do you find that those reservations are not an issue any longer or have they intensified?
- In your marriage, do you face the trials or allow them to accumulate? What can be done to improve in this area?

Father,

Thank you for the gift of marriage! As we journey through this life, may our marriage remain fresh and on purpose. Never let us grow weary of each other and let our love be refueled when we have nothing left in us to give. Remind me of what it means to love and care for my first responder. May our communication never fade, but be constantly renewed.

When trials come, help us to face them with you and not allow accumulation of trials to overtake our marriage. Lord, you be the center of our relationship and our hearts. Let my husband see me, and me see him, through your eyes. I pray we never stop dating each other and become intentional in caring for one another in both good and bad times.

In Jesus Name,

Amen

TRUTH

*Cast all your anxiety on him because he cares
for you.*

— 1 PETER 5:7 NIV

*And let us consider how we may spur one
another on toward love and good deeds,
not giving up meeting together, as some
are in the habit of doing, but
encouraging one another—and all the
more as you see the Day approaching.*

— HEBREWS 10:24-25 NIV

*Be completely humble and gentle; be patient,
bearing with one another in love.*

— EPHESIANS 4:2 NIV

*The LORD God said, "It is not good for the
man to be alone. I will make a helper
suitable for him."*

— GENESIS 2:18 NIV

Love must be sincere. Hate what is evil; cling to what is good.

— ROMANS 12:9 NIV

I NOW PRONOUNCE YOU
HUSBAND AND WIFE

Oh the honeymoon stage in all its glorious wonder! You know, that absolutely perfect getaway time? You are both gleaming and your face announces to the world you are newlyweds. You can't wipe the smile off your face, your life as husband and wife is just beginning, and there is nothing that can stop the two of you. Disagreements? What are those? Ha! Honeymoon phases are wonderful, but they do fizzle out sweet girl. Don't let that discourage you, because now your adventure is truly just beginning.

Marriage has arrived and you will spend numerous years discovering who this man really is, who you really are, and who the both of you are together. People change, people grow, and this is good. The Lord requires us to grow and it is fitting for a husband a wife to complement one another. They are to bring out the best in the other. Officer Uribe and I were doing just that! We were finally together and blinded in our honeymoon bubble. Life was good, marriage seemed to be easy. We were smooth sailing, but as time passed, imperfect moments occurred more frequently.

After five years of arguments, in-law troubles, two babies, and the battle over who squeezed the toothpaste wrong, our journey as husband and wife had officially begun. It was during that time, our marriage seemed to have an uncertain future. It all began with the usual disagreements, but then those differences went into new territory. Petty issues became larger. The more intimate issues left me uncertain as to the future of our marriage. The officer that used to share about his day on the beat was now silent. What we once knew as "us" had grown into a family of four, and although a blessing, it was now a routine.

I could no longer focus solely on him, we had children that needed our attention, and I was pulled in so many directions. As a young wife and mother, there was no balance or hope in sight. There was lack of forgiveness and communication. Our home was filled with irritability, loneliness, and misunderstandings. We were exhausted! This was definitely not what I had planned or expected on our wedding day. So funny how the future seems like a dream in our minds, till we realize it's not.

I came to understand the term "walking on eggshells" – it is a constant echo among officers' wives. When an officer arrives home, his demeanor may vary. His demeanor can be a reaction to what he encountered that day. As officers' wives, we walk on egg shells – almost as if we have to figure out how to care for and help our husbands. It leaves us with many questions and all sense of control is lost. How often have you asked yourself, "Does he need to talk, or to be left alone? Does he need rest, or does he need affection? If I ask about his day, will he respond with more than just a one worded answer?"

I dealt with all of this alone and never thought to pray about it. God was a religion to me back then, and honestly I never really prayed or had the desire to. Even if I had known to pray, sometimes the trials of life can bring us to a numbness. When we feel this way, prayer becomes something we are too paralyzed to do. Of course, I knew in my heart that giving up was not an option.

After all, we were husband and wife; one flesh; and our vows had already been pledged before one another. They were pledged before God in the church, yet God was not a part of my everyday life, much less prayer. Yes, you heard that right. I saw God as a religion I didn't care to partake in, yet I knew prayer is something people do when there is nothing left to do. But instead of turning to God, I took matters into my own hands.

I packed my bags on three different occasions attempting to leave, but never made it out the door. The truth is I didn't want to leave, I wanted to hope. Each time I packed my bags, I yearned for a reason to fight for my marriage and stay. The divorce rate for law enforcement is extremely high and continues to increase. With all my heart I did not want to be another statistic. I wanted to be with my husband and for everything to be okay. Why couldn't all the hurt just go away? It took the third attempt to leave him when the reality of marriage was staring us in the face. The effectiveness of our promises to one another was at its ultimate test. So far, we had failed.

The third attempt, a day I will never forget. It was a day that felt like the end, yet it held more hope than I could have ever longed for. We had a two year old son and a three month old son at the time. My officer was mowing the lawn unaware that I was packing my bags inside. There was something different that day, there was a boldness inside me I had never felt before. I was ready to leave and trust that our separation would be a benefit for the both of us. I put my sons in their car seats and walked toward my husband. "I'm leaving", I said. He said, "Okay, be careful." I said it again, "No, I am leaving you." I began to walk off toward the car and I saw our oldest son waving with a huge smile on his face saying, "Bye daddy! We are going to Grandma's!" Tears began to roll down my face because my son had no idea what was really happening and our 3 month old lay asleep in his car seat. My husband realized this was no longer a threat, but officially happening.

Tears began to roll down his face and he asked me to stay. His eyes looked so desperate and his voice so shaky. He promised he would do what was needed to change and tried to hold me in his arms. I let him embrace me, but my heart felt so far from him. I was exhausted. After exchanging desperate promises and apologies to one another, I agreed to stay. The decision to stay left me so lost and once again wondering how things could ever become better. This was all new to me. I felt stuck.

I reflected back to my childhood. I recalled the times my parents would share when my father arrived home from work. The scene was very different. Our marriage was different. It would take a lot of learning and a lot of forgiving to become stable in our relationship again. It would mean fighting the first responder divorce rate and going against the odds. But, could we do it? I was a wife on duty, but didn't know exactly what that meant. We grow up imagining our wedding day and marriage. If only someone would have warned us about what happens after all the dress up, flowers, and ceremony. That day was a somber one, along the days that followed. But, this is where the beauty of God's work began.

My marriage as a law enforcement wife was about to become the true adventure I never knew I longed for. The one I always imagined, yet it looked so different. Our marriage would go through all sorts of action packed experiences. I'm talking drama, romance, suspense, heart break, and every other kind of wonder you can imagine.

> *"He will give a crown of beauty for ashes, a*
> *joyous blessing instead of mourning,*
> *festive praise instead of despair."*
>
> — ISAIAH 61:3 NLT

As a stay at home wife and sole caregiver of my children, my days were and still are full of laundry, dishes, cooking, and lots of cleaning. It was an afternoon of vacuuming in my living room, when I decided once and for all to talk to God. Sometimes I wonder if I had it out with him that day. I knew of God all my life, but never had a relationship with him. God was someone I went to visit on holidays at our local church. But, during such a difficult time in our marriage, I knew God was a higher power and someone way bigger than me. I knew if I prayed he would listen. Three days after my final attempt to leave my marriage behind, I shut the vacuum off and began to cry out to God. I asked God to save my marriage, to save me, and to change my husband. That was the best conversation I had in all my life with God. I sobbed so hard that I know even my tears spoke out in prayer. There was nothing left in me to say. My eyes were squeezed shut, my face felt swollen, and I could barely breathe through the outpour of tears.

During that time, ashes and mourning seemed to surround me. Oh how I longed for my crown of beauty and festive praise. It was in that moment of surrender that God was permitted to transform my marriage and my life. I realized it wasn't my husband who needed to change; it was me. A decision had to be made in my heart to focus on God and not my circumstances. I wasn't sure what was happening inside me. It was as if hope finally arrived, a hope I could fully depend on. Things were changing inside me. I was ready to discover more about this God I was learning to trust. My eyes shifted to the heavens and off my husband.

That weekend I decided to attend church and gave my life to Jesus Christ. I went to the altar and passed off my marriage, children, and home. These were better off in God's hands and not my own. The pastor called people to the front and I think I ran up there out of desperation. It was like God had been waiting for me my whole life. The pastor extended his hand and gave me the most angelic smile. I poured my heart out to him telling him about the lying I did, the anger inside me, the vengeful heart that consumed me, my marriage, the time I stole a pin from a garage sale, and how God was my only chance at getting through this. I had tried everything, except for God.

The pastor offered a free gift, the gift of salvation. "Salvation?" I asked. The pastor said, "Yes, an opportunity to make Jesus Christ the Lord of your life. It will mean letting go of yourself in order to find who you are in Him. If you decide to follow Christ, he will most definitely transform your life. It will mean you will now have eternal life." It sounded like a pretty great deal! I was losing everything. I took this gift of salvation and found myself feeling freedom. It's hard to explain, but I felt like a new bride that day. It was as if I wore an invisible wedding dress covered in stains. But in my salvation moment, my invisible dress turned white. Transformation was unfolding. Transformation was not instant, but it was the first step getting there. This new life would be the very beginning of so much more to come.

We are brought up to be married in the church, but rarely reminded that our marriage is to reflect the church. My life was once again a new journey, an adventure that went from two to three. This new surrender would require effective promises. It was on! I was ready. Slowly but surely, our marriage went through a process. Although I had packed my bags and left physically, I knew I had packed and left in my heart long before. I knew it was time to start unpacking the junk in my heart, my old way of thinking, and unpack the bitterness I had toward my officer. This led me to some truth that would begin our marital transformation. Giving your life to Jesus Christ doesn't mean you will be problem free, it means you now have a mighty hand to hold onto in this thing called life.

REFLECTION

- Do you feel there are distractions in your life that keep you from seeking God's will in your marriage?
- Have you ever thought of leaving your spouse or are you considering it now? If so, have you considered fully giving it to God and sought his wisdom in your situation?
- Has God been invited into your marriage? Is it a party of two or three?
- Do you see God as a religion or a relationship? Why do you feel this way?

Salvation: have you found it in Jesus Christ?

Father,

Being husband and wife has many challenges. I know that you know my first responder and I for who we truly are. As we love and care for one another, while we may fall short, help us to love one another with a godly love. It is my hope that the both of us would always include you and make you the center. Help us to unpack the junk in our marriage. Give us a hunger to know you and your desire for our marriage. In Jesus name, Amen

TRUTH

"For God so loved the world, that he gave his only Son, that whoever believes in him should not perish but have eternal life. For God did not send his Son into the world to condemn the world, but in order that the world might be saved through him."

— JOHN 3:16 NIV

Therefore, if anyone is in Christ, the new creation has come: The old has gone, the new is here!

— 2 CORINTHIANS 5:17 NIV

Cast your cares on the LORD and he will sustain you; he will never let the righteous be shaken.

— PSALM 55:22 NIV

He will give a crown of beauty for ashes, a joyous blessing instead of mourning, festive praise instead of despair.

— ISAIAH 61:3 NLT

You'll pray to him and he'll listen; he'll help you do what you've promised.

— JOB 22:27 MSG

LOVE IS PATIENT, LOVE IS KIND

Beginning this new journey with Christ allowed me to embrace my role as an officer's wife. As I fought to embrace this new wife on duty identity, there were many obstacles and days that weighed me down. Fear and doubt would stare me in the face almost daily. My mind was a battlefield and victory seemed so far. Where was I to begin on this new found life in God? I longed for a full manual with answers to all life struggles. Then, I remembered. The day I got saved I was handed a bible, but had not yet opened it. It sat on my nightstand collecting dust. Could that be the manual? Was I really ready to open it and understand what it was saying?

Many times we hear how difficult it is to understand the bible, but fail to realize that reading it is a journey to do with God. So, if you think about it, it's almost like reading a language you don't speak, yet in time, you learn. I began by facing one of the challenges in my marriage, love. Searching the internet I typed in, "Love in the bible". With one click it led me to a reality I was not ready to face. I saw the words, "Love is patient, love is kind..." I stopped reading. I sat back in my chair, sighed, and thought, "Here we go. Patient is definitely not who I am, and kind, my actions toward my officer are far from it." There was such a tug in my heart to dive into this word and find out what it meant to me and what it meant for my marriage. Apparently they read it on my wedding day, but I missed it.

> *Love is patient, love is kind; love does not envy or boast; it is not arrogant or rude. It does not insist on its own way; it is not irritable or resentful; it does not rejoice at wrongdoing, but rejoices with the truth. Love bears all things, believes all things, hopes all things, and endures all things.*
>
> — 1 CORINTHIANS 13:4-8 ESV

Now that you have read it, I am sure you are thinking the same thing, impossible! But bear with me. We serve a God who is the same yesterday, today, and forever. There is no doubt that we will change, our spouse, our marriage, but there is comfort in knowing God never changes. So, with that knowledge of an unchanging God, what does that mean for us? God sees ahead, he knows the beginning and end, including in your life. One of the many things I learned was that delay was not denial. Any form of delay I experienced was simply God working things out for the good and our benefit. Learning to love would require patience. Yet, patience was very hard to attain. Praying daily was all I had to hold onto, especially when the challenges came. Some challenges were small, and some big! I realized that although I had given my life to Christ, my faith would have to be put into action and my actions had to be in faith.

Let's start simple. Let's start with naps. My husband loved them, I despised them. I would get so irritated at the thought of his napping. When he would sit in front of the television, I would have an internal fit that exploded on my face. I found my face without a smile and it screamed irritation. My officer would ask simple questions, and I would snap back short answers. Of course, he was not doing anything wrong, I was just dissatisfied that things were not going my way. Let's be real here ladies.

You see, I was living my life in our home caring for our children twenty-four seven without a lunch break. When he arrived home wanting to nap, I thought, "Really? Must be nice to come home and relax. I never get a break!" I was jealous and envious of his rest because I desperately wanted it. Many wives on duty either work inside or outside the home. We all seek rest as human beings, right? It is all about what we are doing and the sacrifices we make. Amidst it all we expect someone to notice our efforts. We want a witness to our struggle and sacrifice, someone to compete with on who should be most tired! I felt lost and couldn't understand. I asked God, "The love for my husband is so far from your Corinthians description. I am not patient, or kind, and I am so jealous of my husband's ability to rest right now." Did God answer? Yes.

One day I was washing dishes when our baby boy started to cry. My husband was napping in the other room, or at least I thought he was. I cradled our son and walked down the hall to a closed bedroom door. I walked in, the room was dark, and my husband lay there bundled in a blanket. I heard sniffling and I said his name. There was no response and I felt numb. In that moment I realized his day was filled with yelling, dead bodies, battered women, abused children, murder, and so much more horrific circumstances.

I got closer and saw tears rolling down his face. I will never know what happened that day, I never asked. However, God knew I needed to see that. His naps were not just rest, they were his opportunity to decompress from such a day on the beat. It was then that my dishes, laundry, cooking, and diaper changing became something I viewed as a blessing. After seeing that, my responses toward my husband began to change. God was molding me. It may have hurt, but it was necessary.

Of course, as wives, we too will face discouragement. We will experience exhaustion and stress from our daily tasks. But after experiencing that moment, I realized the two didn't compare. Rest would mean something different for me, and it would mean something different for him. Rest was something I knew needed to happen if I was going to be an effective wife on duty. We will discuss that later.

Our husbands walk many dark valleys and must cope, or at least find ways to. An officer can come home and take off his uniform, but inside he is still an officer. It's engrained in them, a part of who they are. Inside they fight all they face each day, all while trying to transition to a husband/father role at home. Often, but not always, we may find ourselves expecting them to be something they are fighting to be. We expect them to fulfill their role as our husband and our children's father. Yes, they are called to be just that and should fulfill the oath taken to their family and the badge. However, the stress of the job, along with past experiences, almost create their unexpected response and actions to those they are closest to.

So many people in this world have expectations. Each of us trying to meet them and yet always feel as if we could do more, yet there is no time. The call to duty in a first responder life is one of adrenaline, speed, and hyper attentiveness. They are always on guard knowing they can't rest, not even for a second, because that could be fatal on the beat. They get one call after the other, never fully being able to comprehend or grasp each call.

Trauma after trauma, they go about the beat only to come home and try to shift that guard mode to relaxation. Not easy! Our first responders are like soldiers fighting a war only to come home with those war wounds hidden in their heart and in the deepest corner of their minds. This can cause PTSD, stress, anxiety, depression, sleeplessness, and so much more. After learning this, rest and naps then became something I highly encouraged. I found that a rested first responder was a much better spouse and parent! Just as much as a rested wife on duty is a much better spouse and parent.

Naps were just the beginning and my jealousy was fading away. I found myself preparing the bed for him after work. Was I being kind? Yes! The understanding of rest caused kindness which then took on a whole new level in our home. I began to seek ways to be kind to my officer. Kindness made our marriage all the more interesting. We get so caught up in life and daily activities that we can lose sight of such a simple act. Love is kind! I found myself going out of my daily routine to do extra things for my first responder. I left little love notes in his uniform pocket, prepared his uniform for the next day, shined his boots when I could, and yes ladies, I even laid out the underwear. Spoiled? Maybe, but all I know is this caused a huge shift in our marriage. Acts of kindness caused walls to break down in our hearts, ultimately being the beginning of healing in our marriage. I then read this scripture and it made sense to my heart,

> *Truly I tell you, whatever you did for one of the least of these brothers and sisters of mine, you did for me.*

— MATTHEW 25:40 NIV

This should speak volumes on the treatment of our spouse. Whatever we do for them, we do for God. How can we not be kind, loving, or patient? Of course with all the kind gestures I was showering my first responder with, I also wanted to be shown that same kindness. I loved the feeling of seeing his surprised face or smile whenever I went the extra mile. Until one day this little evil voice was in the back of my mind saying, "You do all these things for him, but what has he done for you?" There was a tug of war in my thoughts, and really one that was in my heart. I had to remind myself that all the acts of kindness was for God, and that all kind acts I did for others meant so much more. I was fighting to live an unselfish life, but that old self seeking mentality wanted to take over again.

Thoughts of unfairness screamed loud, "Why do I have to do everything and get nothing in return?" I asked the Lord to help me understand, but instead he did something else. This was an ongoing battle until a moment at a stoplight changed everything. My first responder was driving one afternoon and when we reached a stoplight he put his hand on mine. I glanced over at him and with a sweet smile he thanked me for being such a great wife and told me how happy I made him.

That moment eliminated all those nasty and selfish thoughts. It was such a special moment I will never forget. That remark meant he noticed. He noticed all those little acts of kindness and that was better than any physical gift I could have received. Want to know what I said when he expressed his gratitude? I said, "You don't need to thank me." Yes, I laughed too, especially coming from the one who was demanding it in my thoughts daily. I must admit, I got lost in the moment. It felt good because not only did it confirm my husband felt loved, but I saw it as a godly reward for putting my faith into action.

Although it showed my husband took notice, it showed me that God saw all of it. You see, we serve

a God who sees everything! He sees you right now!
He has seen all your sacrifice, even the ones others
haven't acknowledged you for. However, in the end I
had arrived to a place where I loved my husband.....
period. It was not for what he could give me, it was
for who he was and that was finally enough. The
tears you have shed, long nights, the worry you face
when late breaking news of an officer appears on the
television, is all seen by God. The love God has for
you is so unconditional, he loves you ...period.

After attaining patience, kindness, and a non-
envious heart, I had to work on my boastfulness.
Being boastful and self-seeking in a marriage can be
so easy. Have you ever reminded your spouse how
you always clean the house, get up with the
children, pay the bills, or have so much
responsibility it feels like you are a single parent at
times? I did! I wanted recognition for all my hard
work. I learned that this boastfulness was so selfish.

I can't tell you how many times I reminded my
officer how hard I worked in the home and it
seemed as if he didn't appreciate it. Funny how I
would tell him he didn't need to thank me in the
good times, yet in the bad I expected it. His face
each time I spoke such boastfulness hurt my heart.
The fact is, I was doing so much, as I am sure you
are too. But the truth is, the both of us were
working hard each day and although I appreciated
all he did, I couldn't even remember the last time I

thanked him or acknowledged him. Who was I to expect when I wasn't even giving him the same credit? The golden rule needed to be sharpened in my home. It hurt to think my officer goes out to serve and protect his city each day without ever receiving recognition or even told, "Thank you."

God's word led me to another truth......

> *Whatever you do, work at it with all your heart, as working for the Lord and not for men, since you know you will receive an inheritance from the Lord as a reward. It is the Lord Christ you are serving.*
>
> — COLOSSIANS 3:23 ESV

All the blessings in our lives are from God. This includes our family, home, job, children, and so much more! These are blessings given to us to care for. If God handed you a beautiful gift, would you throw it away? Mistreat it? Let it gather dust? Of course not! Perhaps if a friend gave you a gift you could possibly re-gift it, exchange it, or even toss it out, but it is so different when it's from God.

It is important to remember how blessed we are. Not lucky, blessed. While caring for our blessings, we must remind ourselves it is all for the Lord. We can choose to see everything as a blessing or an inconvenience. As you journey this wife on duty life, you too must remember what a blessing you are. Your officer and family need you. It is my hope you know how appreciated you are for all you do. It is not just what you do in your household, but in all places you go.

It is a true sacrifice to love. Love is a wondrous gift to be experienced in the form of a journey. The love we give may lack much, but when we put full intention into pouring it out, things begin to transform. Each of us strive for blessings and goodness, but how can we receive when we can't care for what we possess now? The Corinthians description of love goes beyond patience, kindness, envy, and boastfulness.

It makes it clear what love is not, such as proud, dishonoring, self-seeking, not easily angered, never delighting in evil, but instead it rejoices in truth and ultimately perseveres. As one flesh, hurting your spouse would be like hurting yourself. It is so true because when one hurts, the other hurts. When there is an argument, both of you are angry. You two are one. This brought me to the question of how much I loved my officer. How much was I willing to sacrifice? Let me count the ways. My pursuit to love him in such a godly way became a mission. I wanted my officer to know that I would always strive to be hopeful in our marriage and above all, persevere. I had a desire to love him unconditionally. It is so frightening to think my walk down the aisle was led by conditional love. My assumption was he would always remain the same. What I saw and felt before marriage was a permanent thing in my mind, oh how I was wrong. The both of us were seasonal, we would change and transform into who we needed to be for the sake of a strong marriage and each other. Question remaining now is, how much are you willing to sacrifice?

REFLECTION

- Read Corinthians 13:4-7 and write it down. Pray and ask God to help you love in such a way. Ask God what he is revealing to you through this verse.
- Do you see yourself as a person of patience? Recall times in your marriage where your patience was tested, what will you do to ensure you respond in a patient way?
- Random acts of kindness are known to be done for strangers. Practice acts of kindness toward your spouse. Create a list of ideas.
- Do you keep a record of your spouse's wrong doings? If so make a list, surrender it to God and ask him to help you forgive. Once that is complete, toss the paper out!
- What does it mean to you to persevere in marriage?

Father,

I praise you for leaving us with truth in your word. Your faithfulness in all our marital circumstances makes all things possible. I pray that my love shows patience and kindness. Let my officer and children see the love of Jesus Christ through me in both actions and in words.

Reveal any lack of forgiveness in my heart and help me to forgive as you have forgiven me. Help me to forgive in such a way that I keep no record of wrong doing. Let my hands be kind in serving and expressing love. Let your description of love be what I strive for in my marriage. Remind me that no matter what I feel, you are there and you see me.

In Jesus name, Amen

TRUTH

Whatever you do, work at it with all your heart, as working for the Lord and not for men, since you know you will receive an inheritance from the Lord as a reward. It is the Lord Christ you are serving.

— COLOSSIANS 3:23 ESV

*Love is patient, love is kind; love does not
envy or boast; it is not arrogant or rude.
It does not insist on its own way; it is not
irritable or resentful; it does not rejoice
at wrongdoing, but rejoices with the
truth. Love bears all things, believes all
things, hopes all things, and endures all
things.*

— 1 CORINTHIANS 13:4-8 ESV

*Whoever lives in love, lives in God, and God
in them.*

— EPHESIANS 4:2 NIV

I am my beloved's and my beloved is mine.

— SONG OF SOLOMON 6:3 NIV

A GOOD THING

The word of God says, "He who has found a wife has found a good thing and obtains favor from the Lord. (Proverbs 18:22 ESV) So, if your officer has found you, he has found a good thing! Let this bring joy to your heart. As I speak with many wives on duty around the world, I find that each of them are always seeking resources. They seek resources to improve their marriage, help their marriage, or new found knowledge about law enforcement to help them better understand it. These wives, like yourselves, are being effective in their promise as a helper to their officer. After all, it is only natural for you to want to help! The Lord did send your officer his suitable helper.

I know this, you know this, but many of us may never comprehend the full capacity of what this call on our officers truly means. The view from our officer's side will look different from the view of it on our side. Yes, we walk the thin blue line together, but we each bring in our own sacrifices and insights. God has given us two different views because we are two different souls in this marriage/relationship. While our officer sees blood, we see the trauma in their eyes. While they hear the screams, we see their frustration.

When they take a child away from his mother due to arrest, we awake to the restlessness of their night. Our officers witness trauma each day, and as a wives, we witness the various effects of that trauma. Sometimes we may feel helpless or unable to bring comfort. But, may I remind you once again, as I can't stress this enough, you are a good thing in your officer's life. Without you being the helper God has called you to, they could not go out each day and do what they are called to do.

Let's break this down; why are you good?

There are some characteristics we obtain as a wife that can be a blessing, can be a godly example for our officer, and even draw our officer back to the Lord should he get lost.

First and foremost we are called to be our officer's helper. What does this really mean? Many wives on duty mention that at times they feel like a doormat. Wives seeking to help in every way possible while their officer doesn't reciprocate, would leave anyone feeling this way. This leaves many wives wanting to throw their hands in the air and quit. But, hold on, let me explain what being a helper really means. It does not mean you are beneath him or a door mat.

As a wife on duty, you are called to come along- side him to fulfill the purpose or needs the two of you have as a couple. Each of you individually have a calling given by God in marriage. Yes, even the Lord expects your officer to fulfill that call. Remember, marriage requires two, a team. As the famous quote says, "There is no I in team work." You were created to be his suitable helper in this marriage, with the knowledge that God has given you.

You must realize that only you can accomplish this. God created a wife on duty with such unique traits as he knew this marriage would be different. Not every marriage will face what we do as a first responder couple. If you ask the wife of a banker, doctor, or car salesman, you will see just how different and unique being married to a police officer really is. There are certain gifts given as we experience the emotional, mental, or physical needs in our officer. These gifts enable us to fulfill our husband's need for help. You were made to complement him and he was made to complement you.

Even the word of God says,

Two are better than one.

— ECCLESIASTES 4:9

NIV

Reading that scripture that two are better than one brings us to an understanding. With all the things we face in this marriage, understanding is something that is not always easy. Of course we know the beat is a dark place, but to be present in it and experience it for ourselves, now that makes it different. In order for us to be understanding we need to communicate with our officer. If we want to help, we must communicate with the one who needs it.

There have been times in my marriage and perhaps some of you can relate, where my officer comes home and it's a "slam the door" kind of day. He rips the Velcro off exhaling loudly, and I just know his day was not good. Aside from staring at him with concern, I ask him if he's hungry, tired, or needs to talk. Depending on the situation, he will either want a nap, a hot meal if he didn't eat lunch, or he will open up and unload all about his day. But, that's just it, there will be times when we should ask our officer and times where we need to ask God for his guidance.

Remember, they could have just given a death notification an hour before or stood over a dead body while the deceased's family screamed in agony. In this wife on duty life, needs will change day to day and at times hour to hour. God will give you wisdom with insight to see, and a willing heart to fulfill the need. Because you are suitable and called to help him, only you could fulfill such help and call here on this earth.

As wives we are also called to be Prudent. This goes hand in hand with being a helper. As stated in the word, "A prudent wife is from the Lord" (Proverbs 19:14.) Prudent is defined as acting with or showing care and thought for the future. In other words, a wife who is wise, discerning, vigilant, and understanding. Is it just me, or is this a bit comical because of how true these traits are for all of us as police wives?

As with any wife, these characteristics make for a well-planned and holy-spirit led wife on duty. Being a prudent wife on duty can mean many things in any marriage, but it will always be a blessing. Let us think about the care we provide because of the understanding we have about their work. Every wife on duty will help uniquely depending on their marriage and the circumstances. What ties being a prudent wife into our walk, will be the understanding of who we are as we walk the thin blue line. In that understanding and knowledge, we prepare ourselves for many possibilities.

When our officer faces injuries, line of duty deaths, PTSD, or trauma, being a prudent wife will allow us to consider our actions and be proactive in the present, as well as the future. With the knowledge we have as a wife on duty, this insight will be of help to our officer in the care they need at home or in the case they need outside council.

Then, there is submission.

> *Wives, submit yourselves to your own husbands as you do to the Lord. For the husband is the head of the wife as Christ is the head of the church, his body, of which he is the Savior. Now as the church submits to Christ, so also wives should submit to their husbands in everything.*
>
> — EPHESIANS 5:22-24 NIV

Submission has such a bad reputation because it is viewed with the idea that a wife is beneath their husband/officer. No! Once again, submission does not mean you are a slave or doormat to your spouse. If anything we are called to love and serve one another. Remember, love is an action, therefore the love you have for each other should cause the two of you to desire to serve and love one another. Love does not expect, demand, boast, or dictate.

Submission all comes down to respect. As we follow Christ in our lives, we submit to Christ out of pure love, respect, and honor for Him. With the love we have for our officer, why would we not do the same?

Ephesians goes on to share more about marriage and our roles. God designed marriage with your husband as the leader of the home. This means that your officer has the ultimate responsibility for both you and your family. Just like the police force expects him to take authority over his jurisdiction and hold him accountable, the Lord also expects him to take the leadership role in your home and the Lord will hold him accountable. The Lord knows our men may get lost therefore we are also directed as wives to "submit only as is fitting in the Lord" (Colossians 3:18 NIV.)

If your officer leads you to sin or go against the word of God, know that this is not acceptable and you should never do it. There are limits and boundaries when it comes to submission, as well as understanding your officer is not called to command or demand of you. We are always to obey God first and foremost. As the scripture continues we see more of God's call on your officer, and call on the both of you as a couple.

> *Husbands, love your wives, just as Christ*
> *loved the church and gave himself up for*
> *her to make her holy, cleansing her by*

*the washing with water through the
word, and to present her to himself as a
radiant church, without stain or wrinkle
or any other blemish, but holy and
blameless. In this same way, husbands
ought to love their wives as their own
bodies. He who loves his wife loves
himself. After all, no one ever hated their
own body, but they feed and care for
their body, just as Christ does the church
— for we are members of his body. For
this reason a man will leave his father
and mother and be united to his wife,
and the two will become one flesh. This is
a profound mystery—but I am talking
about Christ and the church. However,
each one of you also must love his wife as
he loves himself, and the wife must
respect her husband.*

— EPHESIANS 5:25-33 NIV

As we are called to submit, our husbands are called
to love, give, care, present, and cleanse us as wives.
In police terms, they are to be our "cover". Our
husbands are to cover us and we are to trust their
lead. Our attitude in loving, serving, and respecting
our officer will change our attitude about
submission. We are called to love one another as we
love ourselves and as the Lord has loved us! Loving

in such a way brings about shared love, honor, and respect in both officer and wife. How you ask?

> *Whatever you want men to do to you, do*
> *also to them.*
>
> — MATTHEW 7:12 NKJV

The golden rule! Remember this basic elementary principle? Whatever we desire or want from our spouse, we must do unto them. Jesus laid the foundation for such a principle. He did this by loving us first, that we may love him in return. If you recall chapter four where my mission was to love my officer in such a godly way, it was filled with pure intention. I sought ways to help, I became prudent, and I learned what it meant to submit. In our marriage we must be intentional in caring, we must be proactive in helping, and we must do this "on purpose". Purpose is what makes marriage successful. The two of you were not brought together at random, there is a purpose for you both as a married couple. There is a reason you are his bride!

God knew that in marriage there may be times we find our men not just lost, but in a place where God is not an option. In this line of work even many bible believing Christian officers become lost or give up on their faith. If you find your officer in such a season, I have good news and hope for you. As wives there is a powerful promise in the bible that says,

> *Wives, in the same way submit yourselves to your own husbands so that, if any of them do not believe the word, they may be won over without words by the actions of their wives, when they see the purity and reverence of your lives.*

— 1 PETER 3:1 NIV

This promise blew me away when I was seeking and praying for my officer to desire a relationship with God. There were many days I wanted to quit all this "doing good" and "respecting" him. There were times I felt he didn't deserve all the sacrifice I underwent. What I never understood is how I expected him to act in a godly way, when he didn't even know God. How could I expect a man who barely loved himself, to love me? But, looking back, I praise God I never quit.

I am grateful because marriage isn't about me and marriage isn't about you either. Marriage is for the other and it's for the both of you as one. As I fought for our marriage, everything came against the desire to love my husband in such a godly way. You see, my husband came to know Jesus because I chose to believe the promise God gave me in 1 Peter. I fought every day without words in the actions of love I chose to give. I did this for the sake of my officer coming to know Jesus as His Lord and Savior.

If you ask my husband how he came to know God, he will tell you this, "I wanted what Allison had. I wanted to know that peace and what changed her. I wanted to know what caused her to love me even when I didn't deserve it."

Do you see? The marriage you are in is part of such a massive, bigger picture. This is why God sees you as good. It's not about being a doormat, it's about how capable you are to lead your man back to the arms of Jesus. When your officer sees the darkest hour on the beat and doubts there is a God, he will see the light through you. Should you choose to be an extension of heaven in this world for your family, they will know the way they should go and their faith will be unshakeable. These are just a few of the good things God sees in you, His wife on duty. There is so much more! Just know that no matter what, you are a good thing and because of you, your husband can obtain favor from the Lord.

Being beside the badge where you were called to shows how equal you are to your husband. One badge, one call, one purpose, all while being the wife on duty God has called you to be. Amidst all this, as wives, we can be a witness and an example of God's peace even without words. In our marriage there will be times we fail to ensure our officer is okay. There will be times we know exactly what to do and times we don't. There will be times when silence is golden, and times when words are necessary.

Our arms may be needed for embracing and our hands to wipe tears. Perhaps there may be nights we feel alone with our own sorrow or times where we hold the fort because duty calls yet again. But sweet wives on duty, now is the time to remember that while its two different views, it's always been *one call*. You are in this with your officer. God will give you the wisdom you need. You are good. You are a gift. You are capable. You are appreciated. Most of all, you are suitable!

Could you imagine a day without you? Just imagine with me.

A day without you would be a sad day indeed. Being a wife on duty is not about what you do, it's in what you express to those around you. The nonverbal is so much louder. It's what you do in silence that makes the deepest impact. The things the world will never know. The sacrifice is astounding. The love is too deep to explain. The strength is fierce. But most of all, the women called to this life are set apart.

So what would a day without you look like?

For one, there would be no heart in the home that our first responders return to. There wouldn't be prayers whispered so eloquently and passionately as our first responders head out. The strength needed to uphold our first responders when they need to be held or felt safe, would cease. The touch of your hands that can calm and bring peace would not be there to reach for his. As your voice calms the war or anger inside him, the silence would be too much to bear. But the sacrifices, the one thing that screams *love* would stop. A day without you would be a day without witness.

You are the witness. You see it all. You raise up your sleeves and your arms are full of strength. You listen to the heartache of the beat and embrace a broken heart. As you hear of the officer down while fighting tears, still you let him go. Never doubt your worth. Never assume you are not enough or doing enough. Don't believe that they can do it without you.

If anything, it's the total opposite. For you to stop, would be a day without light. For the strength beside the badge is you. The thin blue line cannot be walked without you. And a day without you, is unimaginable. So as I conclude this chapter, let me say, "Thank you wives on duty." Thank you for all you do in silence, in sacrifice, in hope, in strength, in the seen and unseen, and in love. Thank you for being the good.

Reflection

- How do you view your role as an officer's wife? Do you see yourself as good?
- Submission – is this a struggle for you, if so why?
- Are you intentional in your marriage about how you express love for your spouse and your love for God?
- Look up and write down Psalm 139: 13-14. Place it somewhere that is visible and begin to see yourself through the eyes of God!
- With the promise of 1 Peter 3:1, does it give you hope? Should you choose to hold onto this promise and live it out, keep a journal and write down all God does through you and in your officer!

TRUTH

Then the LORD God said, "It is not good for the man to be alone; I will make him a helper suitable for him.

— GENESIS 2:18 NIV

Your wife shall be like a fruitful vine within your house.

— PSALM 128:3 NIV

Above all, love each other deeply, because love covers over a multitude of sins.

— 1 PETER 4:8 NIV

Be completely humble and gentle; be patient, bearing with one another in love.

— EPHESIANS 4:2 NIV

My command is this: Love each other as I have loved you.

— JOHN 15:12 NIV

Two are better than one, because they have a good return for their labor: If either of them falls down, one can help the other up. But pity anyone who falls and has no one to help them up. Also, if two lie down together, they will keep warm. But how can one keep warm alone?

— ECCLESIASTES 4:9 NIV

THE REAL ENEMY

Our officers patrol the beat each day fighting off evil. They bring peace to chaos, solutions to problems, safety to the endangered, and above all... they guard. The thin blue line divides the good from evil, and there is no difference when it comes to spiritual matters. There is a God and there is a devil, also known as the enemy. There is one who is for you and one against you, making the difference between God and the devil very clear. God has come to bring life and the enemy has come to bring death.

The thief comes only to steal and kill and destroy; I have come that they may have life, and have it to the full.

— JOHN 10:10

What does this mean for us as wives on duty? It means everything. The enemy wants to take so much from you. He wants your marriage, your children, and the list is limitless. In this chapter I want to focus on a few specific targets the enemy has lurked in when it comes to our law enforcement community.

Let's start with the startling statistic in law enforcement marriages. As a first responder couple we are faced with a higher divorce rate that is estimated at 75%. I have found that divorce or separation is common and the numbers are rising. At times we may hear of a couple divorcing and find ourselves saying, "What? I didn't know they were having problems!" OR "But they seemed okay, they looked happy." Truth is, we never know what battles others are fighting in secret. When my husband informs me of a divorce or separation he heard about, it breaks my heart and it should break yours too.

Our officers, both men and women are suffering from post-traumatic stress. Many of our men are being led astray by women other than their wife, addictions, communication is ceasing, love and respect have become conditional, and the strain from long working hours are taking a toll on families. There is one thing we are quick to forget, self- included, and it is the fact that our officer is not our enemy. When we face marital struggles with our spouse, we point our finger at them very quickly. How can we not when we witness them in hurtful behavior? We also forget our own shortcomings. When I say our husband is not the real enemy, here is the proof.

> *For we are not fighting against flesh-and-blood enemies, but against evil rulers and authorities of the unseen world, against mighty powers in this dark world, and against evil spirits in the heavenly places.*
>
> — EPHESIANS 6:12

In the beginning of our marriage I remember battling my officer. I blamed him, condemned him, and at times held him prisoner in my lack of forgiveness toward him. Had I known then what I know now, I would have aimed it all toward the real enemy instead of toward my officer. Of course this wouldn't have changed the anger I felt toward him or resentment at times. However, if I had left it to God and fought the enemy in prayer, there is no doubt God would have helped me with my emotions or responses toward him. As wives, we are quick to pray for protection over our officer, but we must always remember to pray so much more. We should pray for even deeper issues. We must pray for his mind, for his decisions, his discernment, for him to be able to stand against any temptation, and for him to always be led by God alone. In everything we pray, it will always lead back to our heart. True transformation comes from a surrender of ourselves, a willingness to leave our lives in the hands of God.

There was a time when my officer openly admitted to struggling with looking at other women, also known as adultery. He had come home from a faith based retreat designed for first responders. I remember his quiet demeanor when he returned. I assumed it was the peace he felt, but it was really the struggle in his mind to share something he knew would hurt me. The confession he made could have broken my trust. The enemy was wanting him to remain silent and God was wanting him to expose. I can only imagine all the lies the enemy was putting in his head that day. Not to mention, the enemy will do everything to magnify your officer's weaknesses, and vice versa.

My husband asked if we could talk and naturally I dropped everything to listen. I could see seriousness in his face. He began speaking about the retreat and how he prayed for God to help him in a specific area. He felt God wanted him to share this struggle with me so it would no longer be hidden, but exposed. This exposure to his struggle would bring him to overcoming it and his healing. As my officer shared his struggle in adultery, my heart raced. I felt sick to my stomach and tears came pouring down. Internally I prayed as loud as I could. My heart was pleading for God to guard my mouth from anger or words I would never be able to get back. His confession was delicate and fragile. That crucial moment would make us or break us. I had one shot to either ruin his vulnerability in sharing, or to lead him into trust that would give him the courage to be transparent.

He mentioned what he looked at, who he looked at, and how he had a hard time stopping. What happened next was all God, because in my own human ability, I wanted to be cold and angry with him. He kept hugging me and deep inside I wanted him to leave me alone. His touch felt like betrayal. Instead, I grabbed his tear filled face and I thanked him for telling me. I also told him that I was going to pray for God to help him in this area. I promised we would walk this out together. He gave me another big hug and let out a huge sigh of relief. I was crying so much because it hurt, but we both knew we had to cover one another and pray.

After a few minutes, my loose and resentful arms held him tight around his neck. I wasn't completely blind to his struggle, it was just something I feared to confront. There were many times I found pictures of women in bikinis on the computer history search. I would find DVD's in his office drawer that contained pornography. I would read through numerous text messages from officers about the "hot" girl at the restaurant. Of course, I noticed his eyes wonder from time to time. Through it all, I just wanted him to be honest about it. God never intends for our sins to remain in darkness, he wants them exposed and brought to light so we can fight the real enemy in prayer.

Marriage and love truly is a battlefield. What bothered me most is that I too had struggled with adultery, yet thought nothing of it because I wasn't the one who would get hurt. I would look at men and notice the flirtatious stares. At times I would smile back or exchange small talk, but I never had the courage to tell my husband. Those selfish moments gave me a quick ego boost and nothing more. My officer stood before me exposing his sin with courage, and I kept my sin inside like a coward. Of course I eventually told him, and together we became free from adulterous behavior. Truth is, in marriage we are two imperfect people who love imperfectly. Only Jesus at the center can love perfectly through us and lead us into a righteous marriage. No matter what, we can never change our officer. Only Jesus can transform a surrendered heart.

God has such a wonderful plan for your marriage! Yet the enemy has a plan too. This very real enemy will do anything to ensure you both stumble. He wants to keep you in the dark and in a prison of self-pity and condemnation. He wants you to keep a record of all your spouse's wrong doings. The result of living with God at the center allows you to live in freedom and have the opportunity to turn ashes to beauty. For example, when my officer exposed his weakness, the both of us were able to heal, pray, and overcome.

A few weeks after we shared in such a transparent moment, I caught him in his office cutting the DVD's that contained pornography. He threw them in the trash and had taken the next step to be freed from his ways of lust. I often wonder what would have been if I had allowed my anger to take over. What would have happened if I didn't express the grace that led him closer to God and closer to me? What would have happened if God was not in our lives?

Remember when I said that our officers are called to be our "cover"? It's like this, imagine an officer pulling up to a call where gunfire is coming right at him. They are trained to take that enemy down and cover those around him in protection. The enemy will shoot at you both with any weakness he can find. As a couple you should protect one another. As the head of his household, your officer should always be vigilant in covering you as his wife. Covering your spouse will mean prayer, grace, forgiveness, and lots of it.

Our marriages will always need prayer. If your

marriage is healthy and problem free, praise God and pray anyway. If your marriage is struggling, give it to God, and pray diligently. No matter what, always pray and in everything give thanks. Prayer will be what shields you both. It will be your armor. As you pray, grow beyond praying for his safe return and protection. The enemy wants to get your man any way he can. Will you let him have him? I didn't think so. The real enemy wants to kill, steal, and destroy all he can when it comes to your marriage and any other marriage he can get his hands on. He is relentless and therefore you should be relentless in your prayer life.

The heart of your officer will need the most covering. Everything flows from our hearts. He should be able to be around women and not be moved, he should make wise decisions without being careless, he should love you as Christ loves the church, he should be able to be strong in the Lord without your reminders, and he should know His God no matter what comes his way. It will always be a heart condition. Any sinful behavior on his part has nothing to do with you, it has everything to do with his heart not being in right standing with the Lord. Just like your sinful ways have nothing to do with him, but your heart condition.

You are enough, you are suitable, and you are His Mrs. No-one is to blame but the real enemy who attacks the core of our being. The question is, how hard do we want to resist and fight this real enemy? The one thing that will keep us ready and aware is armor. Our officers gear up each day with tools to assist them on the beat. If our officer has gear, so should you. Our battle doesn't just stop with prayer, it starts with gear.

> *Therefore, put on every piece of God's armor so you will be able to resist the enemy in the time of evil. Then after the battle you will still be standing firm. Stand your ground, putting on the belt of truth and the body armor of God's righteousness. For shoes, put on the peace that comes from the Good News so that you will be fully prepared. In addition to all of these, hold up the shield of faith to stop the fiery arrows of the devil. Put on salvation as your helmet, and take the sword of the Spirit, which is the word of God. Pray in the Spirit at all times and on every occasion. Stay alert and be persistent in your prayers for all believers everywhere.*
>
> — EPHESIANS 6:13-18

I remember learning such a valuable lesson from something so random or should I say, simple. We

live in Texas and the heat caused his vest to stink
with all the sweat! I carefully took it apart in order
to wash it, not realizing later would be difficult. I
paid careful attention to detail as this could be life
threatening if done incorrectly. As I carefully placed
the panels back, I ensured it was done precisely and
without any error. This whole washing ordeal had
me stressed to the core. What if I messed up? If
something happened to him, I couldn't forgive
myself. I made my officer inspect it too!

With each panel and Velcro, it was a reminder of our
marriage. Why couldn't I be so delicate with it the
way I was with the Kevlar? So many actions, words,
decisions, or selfish ambition could lead to killing
my marriage. I was no longer careful, but going
through the motions assuming my marriage was
intact and everything in order. The Kevlar shields
any outside weapon or influence. The Kevlar is said
to absorb the impact of a bullet and disperse it
across the panel. The Kevlar makes the hit
ineffective. There is something powerful there. As a
wife on duty, I often wonder if I keep my shield of
faith on. Is my Kevlar strapped tight?

Many bullets may come flying our way in marriage,
but we must be ready, I am talking prayed up and
geared up! When ANY outside hits come into
marriage, let us know we serve a God who does far
more than absorb the impact, He is the impact. I
like to call this the Kevlar effect. This Kevlar effect is

much like marriage. It's a vital part, something that can't be taken lightly. It is a place of safety, something we cling to as hope, and a strong representation of perseverance. Now, do you see the importance of gearing up? It could mean the death of your marriage.

Sweet ladies, our first responders do not walk into situations lightly and neither should you. If anything, they walk forward with caution, wisdom, and with courage. Today be encouraged that while you may physically not have gear, you have a spiritual gear designed to protect you. Be sure to put it on each day asking the Lord to always keep you alert and vigilant. Many times the enemy likes to attack the mind. If he can get there, he can replace truth with lies. But, this is where you need the truth to stand on and realize who you're really battling.

Some of you may be facing a battle right now and you have no hope in your heart. Get your battle gear on! Ladies, we need to fight in prayer each and every day. This is where you say, "NOT TODAY, TOMORROW, OR EVER SATAN!"

Here is a little help.........

Satan,

I write this in hopes that you will fully understand my commitment to God and his faithfulness to me. You have come into my thoughts and twisted them around. I have doubt, fear, uncertainty, and a feeling of being lost. Did you know that God gave me a spirit of joy, peace, and sound mind? Your constant lies may have made me feel defeated and unworthy, but God made me victorious and knows the plans He has for me. His plans help to prosper and not harm me; His plans give me a hope and a future. As for you, you want me destroyed and defeated, but not today, not now, not ever. I have rebuked you numerous times along with all you have tried to do to destroy my marriage, my children, and me. Well, your schemes and deceptions may come and go, but my God remains by my side both day and night. His word remains true and is engrained in my heart. I have hidden his word in my heart, so I will not sin against Him. Don't you see, satan? As for me and my house we will serve the Lord. We will serve the Lord, not you. I am woman of faith, the daughter a King, and I can do all things through Christ who strengthens me. I can cry out to my Jesus and know it reaches His ears. The best part is – when I cry out to him - as long as I have the faith of a mustard seed my prayers will be answered. And satan, I will have the last laugh- the last laugh that will be filled with joy, knowing that God has, God will, and God forever shall be. You see, I am the wife of a police officer, the wife of a peace keeper. I am the wife you need to worry about, because I know how powerful the name of Jesus is. I know how powerful the blood is that was shed for me. I will fight for my marriage, my family, and my life through the power of prayer and the powerful name of Jesus. So, satan, beware of the wife who is known as a wife on duty. My duty is to serve my God and seek him all the days of my life. I will love the man God has called me to help, and make certain that my home will be a home where God is at the center and is glorified.

After reading this, sweet wives, I am sure you get the idea. What we profess and speak will diminish our defeating thoughts. Another battle we fight as a law enforcement family is PTSD and the symptoms that come with it. Post- Traumatic Stress Disorder is a mental condition. This condition leads to a series of emotional and physical reactions for those who have either witnessed or experienced a traumatic event. Our first responders experience traumatic events almost daily. There is not one officer out there who has not responded to that "one call". It is constantly stated by wives that this call to duty has changed their men.

There is a book that has great information on PTSD and it is "Emotional Survival for Law Enforcement" by Kevin M. Gilmartin. I encourage you to read it if you have not done so. This monster we face has taken lives, marriages, jobs, and peace in many first responders. In this broken world people have done the unimaginable to each other and it is our officers who respond to those unimaginable calls. If your officer is facing post-traumatic stress at a higher level than most, be sure to seek help. At times our officers can respond to their day on the beat in unhealthy ways. It can lead to alcoholism, porn addiction, outbursts of anger, depression, suicide, and more. As mentioned at the beginning of this book, if you are in an abusive relationship, please get help and remove yourself from the unsafe environment. Contact your local shelter and police department. Many officers threaten nothing will be done since "they are" are the police. That is a lie! The department must assist you. You can pray and battle as discussed, but you can pray for him from afar and seek the Lord in the steps to take from there.

Speaking of anger. In our home we have faced moments of sudden outbursts of anger and a variety of responses to his day on the beat. On certain occasions my officer could be calm and collective one second, and angry the next. What I have found in these moments is that in the end, it leaves him feeling helpless and awful. One comment I also hear constantly from many wives is that their officer says, "I don't know why I get so angry, it just happens!" This is a very common occurrence in many law enforcement homes. We can thank hyper-vigilance for this! With your officer in such a heightened state, this can lead to outbursts, restlessness, sleeplessness, and it will show up in their behavior. You, along with your officer, should not feel alone. This does not excuse poor behavior, if anything you and your officer need to discuss healthy solutions and boundaries. As a wife on duty I have learned to recognize my officer's behavior patterns and according to what I see, I am able to help as best I can. One thing I cannot encourage each of you enough in this life is to be the helper God has called you to be. Our officers may not even realize it at times when they have pushed limits that are not healthy.

I remember one evening my officer pulled up and our boys were outside playing basketball with friends. He greeted our boys with kisses and then in a stern voice asked, "Why are you all throwing the ball like a football? Is that a football?" His voice was raised in such a stern officer tone and the kids were suddenly quiet. I heard, "No sir." Then he responded, "Then, play right." Just in the sound of his voice along with the quietness outside, spoke volumes of his day. He came inside, threw his keys on the table, and kissed my daughter and I without saying a word. He slowly walked up the stairs and each step screamed frustration. My daughter looked at me and said, "Bad day I guess." I gave her a gentle smile and told her to wait while I went to check on him.

As I entered the bedroom I asked if he needed anything. He shook his head and stayed quiet. I left the room and prayed for God to bring peace to him and to help me, help him. I waited for ten minutes outside our room and then decided to go back in. When I walked in he was on the floor with his head down. I got on my knees, rubbed his back, and kissed his head. He started to cry silently. I will spare each of you what he saw that day, but you can only imagine. It involved a baby. He was able to share what happened and after some quiet time alone, he was ready to join the rest of the family for dinner. Of course, he apologized to the children for his crankiness. However, they knew it was something he dealt with at work. They understood and loved on their daddy.

You see, in this life, it is not just us who witness the effects of the beat, our children do too. How can we think there is no battle? No matter what our officer's face, it does not excuse unhealthy behavior. I cannot stress that enough. Our marriages must have boundaries and communication. If we find ourselves unable to help, we must seek healthy assistance from our department, counselors, a ministry, or organization.

With the many trials we face in this wife on duty life, at times it is hard to keep peace. Peace – the enemy loves to tackle this one. The late breaking news, the shooting in progress, the officer's down growing in numbers, the riots or protests, it is no wonder peace is a struggle. Fear has become a main factor in our wife on duty journey. But we must remember, fear is a choice. As wives of law enforcement officers there is the one basic fear of the unknown. For one, there is the unknown of his safe return or the close calls we may know of and not know of. There is uncertainty with the public and their reaction toward our family. We witness the hatred directed toward our officers and the rare case of someone threatening our family. Unfortunately, I am sure there are more fear factors I failed to mention. However, let's not focus on what we fear, let us focus on what we can do to stare it in the face. The enemy can work in the craziest and sneakiest ways to ensure fear does not leave you. He wants you in a place of no peace and lack of trust in God. One specific area he aims to gain is in the core of our thoughts. If the enemy can get there, he can get anywhere in your life. You know what I am talking about. The times when doubt enters and you question things. It could also be restless thoughts leading you out of a place of peace.

> *For God has not given us a spirit of fear and timidity, but of power, love, and sound-mind (self-discipline). 2 Timothy 1:7 NLV*

Did you read that? Read it again. You sweet girl, when in Christ, have not been given a spirit of fear or timidity. You have been given the opposite. You have been given a life filled with power in Him, reckless and unconditional love, and a peaceful mind that abides with the mind of Christ. We must learn to recognize when the enemy is seeping into our thoughts and put a stop to it! There is fear and there is wisdom, choose wisdom.

One specific thought I want to set a straight record on is "doormat". How many of you have ever felt that you are a doormat when it comes to fighting for your marriage? Your identity is not in what you do, it is in Jesus Christ. If you do not know who you are in Jesus, you will not know who you are in all things. Come to know God and his purpose for you as an individual. Your identity is not just police wife, mom, sister, neighbor, daughter, co-worker, and the list goes on. Your identity is in Christ who has called you by name. Fighting the enemy will be hard, but we must remember that while we have much against us with the enemy, we have even more for us in Jesus Christ.

As a wife, can you name someone else who will rise up to battle in prayer for your officer with such passion? No. You are called and enough to be the helper God has called you to be. The strength the Lord gives you is far from being a doormat. You are held up. There is power in praying and believing for the best in your marriage. It is not a weakness. In your marriage no one should fight alone. Read your bible, the victory is won, end of story.

Fighting this very real enemy is not a game or fairytale. It is a real battle with real warfare armor. As you pray daily, dress yourself up in the armor of God. As your officer dresses in his physical gear, pray the armor of God over him too. By doing this, you will cover him in prayer internally and externally. Our battle fighting and the way we recognize it will bring us to healthy action instead of destructive reaction. It is better to act upon than to react without wisdom. The enemy should not be something we fear, but something we realize has no authority. We should learn to laugh in joy at his many failed attempts. We should praise God for the victories won and yet to be won. So are you ready to fight? That's my girl! Lastly, since we are a blue family, let us check on one another and be there for each other. Encourage each other in this blue line walk. Pray not just for your marriage, but all marriages. Be a listening ear and a safe place for someone in need. Take advantage of conferences, workshops, retreats, or getaways that will strengthen your marriage. Perhaps give a gift card to another Law Enforcement couple for dinner or a movie. Pour into marriages around you.

Also, don't wait till you have problems to pour into your marriage, always find ways to nurture it. Don't stop dating each other and let your "I love you" be said more than often. Don't forget why you said "I do". Marriage is not easy, it is not a movie experience like "The Notebook". Marriage is full of joy, sadness, anger, excitement, hurt, healing, pain, and happiness. It's an adventure to be done with God at the center. So wives on duty, not a single one of us knows what goes on behind closed doors. If anything is going on behind closed doors, let it be prayer for first responder marriages and your families. Be a couple's miracle, share hope, and may we all be ready to battle the real enemy.

REFLECTION

- Have you ever considered who the real enemy is?
- It is hard to remember the real enemy we battle when angry or hurt by our spouse. What steps can you take to remind yourself that we battle principalities?
- Read Ephesians 6:12 NLT "For we are not fighting against flesh-and-blood enemies, but against evil rulers and authorities of the unseen world, against mighty powers in this dark world, and against evil spirits in the heavenly places." After reading this, pray and ask God to speak to you and show you what he means in regards to this scripture. What does this verse mean to you and how will it change your perspective?
- When dressing in the morning, do you honestly remember to pray and ask the Lord to dress you in the armor of God? Write Ephesians 6:13-18 on a post it and place it in your closet or on your mirror to remind you daily to be battle ready!
- Since law enforcement marriages face such difficulty, ask the Lord to lead you in

pouring into another LE marriage. Whoever
the Lord puts on your heart, bless them
with a night out for dinner, movie, or maybe
even encouraging books that will feed their
marriage as a couple and individually.

- Write down any struggles you may be facing
in your marriage. Look up scriptures to
stand on and speak the truth over those
struggles. Document any changes you see as
you believe the Lord to intervene.

Father,

I praise you for the victory I hold in you. As
challenges come, let me not be quick to grow angry
or become defeated. Give me the strength to turn to
you and pray continually. Dress me in the full armor
of God that I may stand strong against the tactics of
the enemy. As I place your word in my heart, help
me use it boldly against all that comes against me.
Give me wisdom to know how to pray for situations
I encounter and to maintain joy in you. As my
officer goes out on the beat, ordain his every step.
Lead him to desire a relationship with you and make
you his Lord and Savior as you are more powerful
than any Kevlar. I pray that no weapon formed
against me or my family shall prosper. I pray you
will silence the deceiving tongues and that your
word be echoed in all we do and say. Let our mind
line up with yours Lord. Most importantly, we

praise you for fighting our battles and working all things together for our good.

In Jesus name, Amen

TRUTH

Let the morning bring me word of your
unfailing love, for I have put my trust in
you. Show me the way I should go, for to
you I entrust my life.

— PSALM 143:8 NIV

And blessed is she who believed that there
would be a fulfillment of what was
spoken to her from the Lord.

— LUKE 1:45 ESV

For God has not given us a spirit of fear and
timidity, but of power, love, and sound-
mind (self-discipline).

— 2 TIMOTHY 1:7 NIV

Therefore, put on every piece of God's armor
so you will be able to resist the enemy in
the time of evil. Then after the battle you
will still be standing firm. Stand your

*ground, putting on the belt of truth and
the body armor of God's righteousness.
For shoes, put on the peace that comes
from the Good News so that you will be
fully prepared. In addition to all of these,
hold up the shield of faith to stop the
fiery arrows of the devil. Put on
salvation as your helmet, and take the
sword of the Spirit, which is the word of
God. Pray in the Spirit at all times and
on every occasion. Stay alert and be
persistent in your prayers for all
believers everywhere.*

— EPHESIANS 6:13-18 NLT

*Submit yourselves to God. Resist the devil,
and he will flee from you.*

— JAMES 4:7 NIV

*You are from God, little children, and have
overcome them; because greater is He
who is in you than he who is in
the world.*

— 1 JOHN 4:4 NIV

A STORY FOR IMPACT

Each and every one of us have a story to tell. Right now, you may have many stories of victory, loss, joy, sadness, or redemption. But could it be possible you are in the middle of your story? Not just any story, your marriage story. You see, right now as each of us live out this wife on duty journey, we have hope. Yet, some of you may have lost that hope. The truth is that there is not one single perfect marriage out there.

Although you may see the numerous photos on social media sites filled with pristine Christmas photos of families, perhaps the delivery of roses on Valentine's Day, or even that dinner date night, you must remember that each person has a story. Each marriage you are surrounded by has experiences they may not want to share. But, what if we shared our marriage story, not just the great times, but the hard times?

And they have defeated him by the blood of the Lamb and by their testimony.

— REVELATION 12:11 NLT

I remember one Valentine's Day, I posted a photo of my officer coming home with roses on social media. I was gleaming with pride and my heart was full. I believe with all my heart that their uniform does something to a girl. After posting it, I recalled the times he would show up empty handed. For many years, deep in my heart I just wanted to be acknowledged on this commercial day. I would scroll on social media witnessing all these acts of love my friends were experiencing and all I could do was cry and ask, "How come he didn't get me anything?"

Thing is, our marriage was not always like that special moment I posted. It took years to get there. I'm talking packing my bags to leave along with having fight after fight. We went through the first responder marriage struggles. We faced seclusion, anger outbursts, sleepless nights, women who loved his uniform, texts from officers to my husband about the "hot" girl they saw, financial struggles, and more.

This marriage took time and we are still choosing to

say "I do" each day. We went from having an unhealthy marriage to inviting Jesus in. The difference is evident. You see, Valentine's Day can be a day of expectation, yet if we look deeper, it has nothing to do with the roses or chocolate.

It has everything to do with our certainty in knowing we are loved. This is not just on days like Valentine's, it is each day we wake up to spend forever with the one our heart chose. The difference now is, that day I did not expect him to show up with roses, and if he didn't, it would not have changed the fact that I love this man. He has not always shown up looking so sexy in uniform with roses.

In fact, there were days he showed up grumpy, angry, ungrateful, or even bitter in uniform. But back then, even without the roses on Valentine's or any other day, I loved him anyway. Even now, he may show up with no smile and grumpy, but I "still do".

Our stories in this life will not only be different, but they have the ability to be impactful.

> *And we know that for those who love God*
> *all things work together for good, for*
> *those who are called according to his*
> *purpose.*

— ROMANS 8:28 ESV

This particular promise gives such a hope that even in our brokenness, God can cause all things to work together for our good. How many times have you ever felt alone in your struggles? How many times have you felt as if you and your officer were the only people facing the struggle? Truth is there are thousands of people right now facing something similar or identical to what you are dealing with. If we would stop trying to conceal what is failing in our marriages, we could uncover it and seek help in the right places.

Many of our officers fear admitting to a struggle as they are called to be the ones in authority and bring solution, peace, and "fix" any situation. Some see it as a weakness. The realization they face when something is affecting them may lead them to a denial. They may think, "Not me, I don't have problems. I am not like that and don't need counseling. I am not that bad. I can't ask for help because I could get fired."

As for us wives, we too may not be willing or wanting to face what we know could be or is an issue. We must be watchful in our homes.

> *She carefully watches everything in her household and suffers nothing from laziness.*
>
> — PROVERBS 31:27 NLT

So you are probably asking, why do I have to be the one to be watchful? Why do I have to initiate it all? It has nothing to do with you being the one to do everything. As wives we have a heart of discernment that arises in us when any of our children or officer is hurting, angry, resentful, or joyful. We are the heart of our family, the nurturer. As wives we should be encouraged by the promises of God, while allowing discernment given by the Holy Spirit to lead us.

As we are watchful and in prayer, the Holy Spirit will do any convicting. As wives it is not our job to take over the Holy Spirit's role, instead we must pray and then trust the Holy Spirit to fulfill what Jesus promised He would do. When we do this, miracles happen and testimonies are born, allowing our marriage story to be impactful to those around us. In that, our marriage becomes a light in a dark world.

My marriage story has been shared over the years, but I will never forget the moment the Lord showed me what it was to be impactful. I was at a mall, window shopping, when a woman walked toward me. I assumed she was another shopper, but then she smiled hesitantly and said, "Excuse me." She looked at me in a state of disbelief and told me she felt the need to talk to me. She apologized for the intrusion and then said although we knew nothing about each other, she wanted me to know she was having marital issues. Many thoughts went running through my mind, and in my heart, I knew this was no accident.

It was a divine appointment and an opportunity for me to glorify God for his holy works. This was a time to share my story and be impactful in this stranger's life. I assured her it was okay that she approached me and I would listen to her story. She proceeded to tell me that her husband had run off with another woman and was seeking a divorce. She cried all while telling me how much she loved him and how she did not want a divorce. She wanted to believe that they would somehow reconcile. I wanted to tell her about what God had done for me, but I knew at the moment I needed simply to listen.

She repeatedly said how she felt all would be well, but was not sure what it meant. It was in that moment I told her about my marriage, without offering too much detail. My marriage had its struggles, but I could not relate to her situation in any way. I simply asked her one question. I asked if she was a person who prayed and had a belief in God. She looked at me with such a straight face and seemed uncertain of how to reply. She said she had not prayed about it, but she would start to. I told her how important it was to leave it in God's hands, and that when I did, God transformed my marriage.

At the time I was still timid about praying in public

or even with someone. However, I knew there was a reason God had placed us together. I took the deepest breath and asked if I could pray with her. Her face was priceless! Although she looked surprised, she gladly accepted. I was surprised myself as we stood in the middle of a crowded mall with many people passing by. It took courage to do that, which is why I share this story with you. Have the courage it takes to reach out. Once we finished our prayer, I gave her a big hug and told her I would continue to pray for her and knew God would do something great. After all, he works all things together for our good.

After that day I prayed God would take this life of mine and make me a vessel to do his work. I wanted to testify and encourage other women. I told my officer, "There has to be other wives like me out there. Crying themselves to sleep at night, wanting to give up the way I did, or so lost and hurt." Months went by and so many more divine appointments occurred. I kept thinking of how lonely I felt and thought not one person understood. I thought it would be great if four to five wives could join me for a bible study or just get together. I had no idea where to start. I shared my ideas for ministering to officer's wives with my husband and he encouraged it. There was also one problem: I didn't know anyone.

After a year passed I was still dreaming of this bible

study and decided to speak with our church. I was filled with so much vision in my heart and with the pastor's full support, I went ahead and began the process. It turned out there was only one police wife the pastor knew of in the church. No matter what, that filled me with joy.

It was a start! My pastor gave me homework; he said to come up with a mission statement and a name for what would be a small group in our church. I prayed about a name for days and as my patience grew thin I asked my officer what he thought I should call it. He blurted out, "Wives on Duty." I was excited and now I officially had the name along with a mission to support, encourage, and inspire wives of law enforcement and emergency personnel through the word of God. Although I had one member for a year, it didn't matter because I knew what God had called me to. A couple of years went by, and one wife grew into two, and then two into five, then forty-five, and now, there are too many to count. You see, each day holds a ministry opportunity, moments where we can make an impact. God doesn't use the qualified, he uses the willing.

Have you overcome an obstacle in this wife on duty life? If so, how many of you not only overcame, but now want to take that blessing and now be a blessing to others. Are you the one who wants to take your story and reach others in hopes it will encourage them into their own victory? If there is a

stirring in your heart as you read this, it is because the pain you endured was not in vain. We learn in our trials and we grow from them.

Many of you ask, "Where do I begin? What if I'm criticized? How do I reach others?" Or the common phrase, "I know I am supposed to reach out to others, but I keep putting it off." So many ministries, books, blogs, social network sites, or organizations need to be birthed. Perhaps someone out there is experiencing that trial you overcame and is waiting to hear what God has to say through you. Maybe they can't sleep and find themselves praying for direction. The Lord will use you and can use you to share what they need to hear. Even the word of God says we shall overcome by the word of our testimony. If this speaks to you, I praise God for it. He is waiting for the willing hearts to say, "Here I am, send me". To be impactful will mean having vision as your heart is willing.

> *And the Lord answered me: "Write the vision; make it plain on tablets, so he may run who reads it. For still the vision awaits its appointed time; it hastens to the end—it will not lie. If it seems slow, wait for it; it will surely come; it will not delay.*
>
> — HABAKUK 2:2-3 ESV

It is important to remember perfection in this life doesn't exist, but imperfect people loving perfectly can only be done with Jesus. Embrace your story. Be impactful. Create and write out a vision for your marriage. Where do you see yourselves in the future? What is your mission statement? Write down the vision in your heart and wait for it. When we married our spouse, there was purpose, dreams, goals, desires, and all of that was a vision. Don't lose sight of the vision in your marriage. In the meantime, reach for hands that are reaching out. Should the need arise, reach out for hands when you need it most.

REFLECTION

- What does the phrase "A story for impact" mean to you?
- Being impactful does not always mean starting a huge organization, it can be done in many ways. How will you impact police wives or the police community around you?
- Would you say you allow the Holy Spirit to lead your marriage?
- Have you ever thought about another marriage when you see their photos on social media? Without knowing their story, many of us assume it is always great, when

in fact it is not. What do you believe gets our marriage from struggle to victory?

- A mission statement is always wise to have when moving toward a goal. Write a mission statement for your marriage and for yourself.
- Whether or not your marriage is struggling, write down a vision for your marriage. Where would you like to be as a couple twenty years from now?

Lord,

We thank you for vision. We praise you for giving us beauty for ashes no matter where our story is in life. We trust that you will ordain our steps when we leave our life in your hands. Guide us as we journey this life. Allow us to be a light to those around us in the law enforcement community.

Prosper our marriage and come to the center of it. May all we do to love one another be a reflection of you and your unconditional love. Let your will become our purpose. Let our marriage make an impact to those who witness our vow to one another.

In Jesus name,

Amen

TRUTH

Let the morning bring me word of your
unfailing love, for I have put my trust in
you. Show me the way I should go, for to
you I entrust my life.

— PSALM 143:8 NIV

Therefore go and make disciples of all
nations, baptizing them in the name of
the Father and of the Son and of the
Holy Spirit, and teaching them to obey
everything I have commanded you. And
surely I am with you always, to the very
end of the age.

— MATTHEW 28:19-20 NIV

And then he told them, "Go into all the
world and preach the Good News to
everyone."

— MARK 16:15 NLT

To all who mourn in Israel, he will give a crown of beauty for ashes, a joyous blessing instead of mourning, festive praise instead of despair. In their righteousness, they will be like great oaks that the LORD has planted for his own glory.

— ISAIAH 61:3 NLT

You saw me before I was born. Every day of my life was recorded in your book. Every moment was laid out before a single day had passed.

— PSALM 139:16 NLT

OUR HEAVENLY SUBSTATION

M illions of officers report to duty each
and every day at their substation. This
serves as a place of preparation for
them. In there, they gear up mentally, physically,
and emotionally. In the substations roll call occurs,
vital information is shared, assignments are given,
and then they head out onto the city streets.

While our marriage story can be used to make an
impact in the world, our impact should always begin
first in our homes. Why? Because our first ministry
truly begins in the home with our family. This call to
duty does not define our home, yet it is a part of
each life born into it. It's not to overtake us, it's to
sharpen us, to be a stepping stone. Our homes
should equally be a place where we can gear up
before we head out.

It's no secret our husbands have a hard time transitioning from uniformed officer to their family role. While they may remove their duty gear on the outside, their mental and internal gear remains on the inside. When we step back, we notice that they go from one substation to another. I like to think of our home as a heavenly substation, a safe place from a chaotic world.

As law enforcement wives, each of us may run our households in a unique way. With different departments, schedules, and family structure, it will look different for each us. It is about finding what works! Our home has cameras at every corner and four locks on the front door. Our side gates are bolted shut and best of all there is a security system. Our household is guarded like Fort Knox and protected physically. However, I frequently remind myself I need to do all needed to protect it spiritually, emotionally, mentally, and more. We must make our homes a sanctuary, a place of rest.

When our officer's come home they want a place to decompress. This means residing in a stress free home, one with order and structure, and a place where they can take off the badge and be who they really are. They are not the only ones who need it, we need it too. We can have all the physical protection in the world, but if we do not have healthy relationships and boundaries for our marriage and household, we miss the point. Lets' begin with the front door.

The front door is the most important part of your home. Guests come through there, greetings take place, his role as officer stops there, his role as husband and father begin there, guarded hearts come down, and all of you are able to walk through it and simply "be". Yes, I am mentioning a lot of what our officers need, yet you will find that in reality, your whole family needs to find your home as being a safe place too. Whether you work in or outside of the home, you need to be able to return to a place of peace and rest. Homes should not just be a structure with rooms, they should be places of transparency, rest, safety, calmness, and so much more. I recently mentioned to my officer once that my dream home was never about physical structure, but about an intimate one. While the front door opens up to welcome others, it equally shuts out the rest of the world. This allows your family to be in a place of intimacy. Especially being a first responder family, protecting our family time is a must.

Remember the scripture in Proverbs 31:27? It mentions a wife watches everything in her household. Let's dive in to that again and find out how it can relate to our front doors. As we walk through them, our moods come in with us. The day and all its cares have a way to seep in and set the tone in our homes. Not just us as wives, but our officers too. I never realized just how much we can truly set the tone in our home.

There was a day when I woke up with my officer lying beside me and I knew he was supposed to be at work. Surprise! I learned later he was sick all night. Despite the plans on my agenda, I knew I had to press on. I went through the regular morning routine and was feeling pretty good. I had worship music on and as my officer got settled with his blanket on the couch, he mentioned just how peaceful it felt. Once I left the house, the day really took over and my peaceful mood was drifting away. I had to grade the kids school work, buy soccer cleats and shorts, pick up boxes, pick up books, go to the bank, go to the store, cook dinner, and head to soccer practice! Yes, I know, I was exhausted physically and mentally. The day got the best of me.

As I prepared dinner, my very congested husband walked in to apologize for not washing the dishes. I was restless and this was causing him to be restless too. He stood in the kitchen watching me slam cabinets, snap at the children, and toss food around as I spilled it on counters and floors. I was a mad woman. I kept insisting he rest and sit on the couch, but he said, "I can't rest seeing you like this." My oldest son even mentioned how he felt so rushed all day. I felt awful. I allowed the busyness of the day to control me and the tone of my home. I remembered that my peace, and decision to keep it, will affect my household. Our actions, responses, or mood sets the tone in our day and bounces off to those around us. How we walk through the front door can make a great impact or a bad one.

We all know the infamous phrase, "If mama ain't happy, ain't nobody happy." Oh how true that statement is. It is my hope and prayer to be a peaceful vessel as I enter and exit our home. Let us pray God give us all the grace needed to fulfill our daily duties both inside and outside of it. Should we fail, we must be gentle with ourselves, have grace for our heart, and remember we are trying our best. On the flip side, we can experience the effects of the beat and our officers can affect the tone as well. As we go through these experiences you can clearly see it is not just about husband and wife, it is about the children too. One call and one purpose for the whole family.

One day, my officer and I were alone in our bedroom. He sat next to me with concern. My thoughts were racing and tears ran down my face. The stress of the week was catching up to me. I told him, "I really need you to pray over me." He asked, "Why? What's so bad? I thought you were fine. You seemed okay when I got home." I kept crying. I told him with frustration, "I would just appreciate it if you would pray. You forgot to pray over me last night after I asked." He apologized and said he didn't mean to forget, yet he sat there motionless. I looked over at him and realized....he can't pray. "You can't pray right now, can you?" I asked. He nodded his head and I knew his heart wasn't right. The Lord was dealing with me and while I was needing prayer, God led me to pray for him. Funny thing was I sat there frozen, internally fighting whether to pray or not. But I could hear so loudly as the Lord spoke, "PRAY OVER HIM". I got on my knees and began to pray. I held him in my arms and cried out to God for his day on the beat. I prayed about all he saw and heard, for our marriage, and for God to refresh us both. I held him in my arms and reminded him that he never has to do this alone. Something powerful happened. Peace overtook us. We both had tear filled eyes. He kissed my forehead and we shared a smile. Peace had arrived and we received what we both needed.

You see, when we are watchful in our home and need something, we need to do something. What do you do? Let God take over. Seek what the Lord would have you do and watch what happens. No matter the day or week you have had, allow God to refresh you both. When he can't pray, you pray. Let us also keep our hearts in right standing. Sometimes it takes our hands reaching for his, and that takes us to moments in our home where the simple things can be huge. Its moments of surrender that lead to compassion, and that compassion leads to a peaceful setting. We must strive to have a strong prayer relationship with God because this life is filled with chaos or crazy schedules. Don't forget, the battle is on.

Our officers are known to experience a higher level of chaos on the beat. If you think about it, why would the both of you want to go from chaos to chaos? Being watchful goes beyond knowing all activity: it is seeing to it that no matter the amount of activity, a set peaceful tone is established. Both of you are human and will have days of discouragement or frustration, but the outcome of your day will depend on how you handle those days. You have to ask yourself, "Is this a bad day? Or am I having a bad moment?" This is why a relationship with Jesus Christ is so important. It is not a problem free life. Having a God who guides and gives us grace with reckless love, truly sets the tone for all our days. With God we have something bigger than ourselves and are able to be hopeful no matter what comes our way.

In our home we are able to see our officer beyond what the community sees. He is more than just a number on a badge. He has a name, he has a family, his own dreams, and aspirations. He fights battles no other dare approach. He has a goal to come home safely each day. He is loved, honored, and respected. The best part, they are ours and we are his. I remember watching the news one day and it was filled with protests. Sign after sign screamed anti-police. Then, out of nowhere a sign ordering death to our officers around the nation showed up on the screen. In that moment I was filled with anger and rage. I was safe inside my home and each time I stepped out, I felt as if I was hated too. The way I see it, what they do to our men and women in blue, they do to us as well. My teenage son saw one his favorite football teams kneeling against police and as I watched his crossed arms and heavy breathing chest rise, he turned the television off and stomped upstairs. The hatred and division made its way inside our home. I had so much inside me I wanted say, so I wrote it out on paper. Here it is.....

> *Hey you, yeah you, the one holding the sign that says kill more cops! I'm the wife of one of those cops that you want to kill. Every single day I wake up to kiss my officer goodbye and let him go out the door to serve the city that he swore to Serve and Protect. That includes you. While you're holding your sign up declaring to take his life, the life of my husband, he would do anything to ensure that you're safe while you hold up that sign. He would even give his life for you. Did he sign up for this? That statement you make is actually a question to me. No they do not sign up for this and I'll tell you exactly what "this" really is. You see, he didn't sign up to be thrown into a pit where he is judged, he didn't sign up to be spat upon or*

*screamed at in the face while you protest. He
didn't sign up to take a bullet and leave his
family behind. He signed up and swore in
because he knew no other way to live the life he
was called to. A life of sacrifice and to lay his
life down for what he believes in and that is
peace. You see, the line that my husband walks
divides the good from the evil. The line that he
walks is not one that he walks alone because
while you think your hatred is geared towards
him alone, it is ultimately geared toward me
and my children. Yes, me, his wife and his
children. Sure I see all the comments as I scroll
through Facebook and I see all the posts that
are made along with the jokes, your hate, and
your opinion. Does it bother me? Why of
course it does, I'm only human. But here's
where you fail and you don't have me.*

*Listen, and listen good. You will never be
permitted to put fear in my heart or in my
children. You will never have the right to think
you have won if my husband were to ever be
taken from me due to hatred or because he is a
police officer. You will not put me in so much
fear that I feel the need to hide my face or hide
my family. Sorry, but not today or not ever.
I've always thought about what I would say if I
ever saw you face to face holding your sign up
with such hatred in your heart. It became easy*

when I met somebody that actually felt the way you do. Countless wives and family members face you every day. My eyes fill with tears not because of my officer or anything that you have done, but they fill with tears because of the sadness in my heart for you. For you to choose a life of hatred I question if you will ever taste pure love.

So here is what I would say to you or do for you. I'm going to pray for you, because while my husband is out serving and protecting the very City he resides in, I chose to walk this line with him and I walk it proudly. Because I believe in what he's doing I'm going to pray for you. While he's standing there with his gear protecting those who wish him dead, he never runs and hides. You know what he does? He gets up every single day leaving his family behind, that's me and that's my children, knowing full well he may not come home. Sometimes I don't get it, but I get to witness it and it's powerful. It is my hope that you never need him because you're in a state of pure emergency.

Yet if you ever needed him you can guarantee he'd be right there. You do anger me when you have those signs and you post those things of hatred towards those who are serving and protecting you. While I may be angry towards

*it and seriously disgusted, I will never let you
have the core of me. You cannot have my joy,
my peace, or my hope. I hold weapons you have
yet to meet. I have an armor that can
withstand anything, including you. Most
importantly I have a God who sees you. My
God died on a cross loving people like you,
having Grace towards people like you, and
showing compassion towards people like you.
Therefore, I will do it too.*

*Lord knows I can't do it in my own strength,
but I can do it with his strength. So while I
hope you stop doing what you're doing, I don't
expect my words to change anyone's mind or
my opinion to move anyone, but as for me and
my house we will serve the Lord. But as for me
and my house we will serve and protect the
community we are sworn to. Don't you forget
it's not just him, it's his family too. We have
never needed your approval because this is
what sacrifice looks like. This is the thin blue
line. We don't March around it, we walk it.*

— A POLICE WIFE AND HER
CHILDREN

We should often step back and be watchful. As a law
enforcement family there are so many ways for the
chaos of the world to enter our homes. This can

happen in the most unexpected ways. It is important to set ourselves to a Christ-like mentality and further ourselves to an orderly life physically, mentally, spiritually, and emotionally. Yes, I know it is not easy. As a matter of fact, I am still trying to take baby steps in that direction. It takes being intentional and action toward whatever goal you seek to create in your heavenly substation. In doing this we also train up our children to have households of safety for their families as well.

We set the example, the tone, and standards. Nothing should rob us as wives from taking time to ensure our family is top priority. This goes for our officer's too. We must have that vision for our family. So, I ask you, what keeps you from being the wife on duty or mother your household needs? What is keeping your officer from taking part in his family role?

For example, I am on the computer or phone quite often tending to the ministry or responding to messages. My husband came into the room one day and said, "Oh, you're on the computer." Now, these words may sound harmless, but it was the sarcasm in his voice that got my immediate attention. I stopped what I was doing and went to ask if he was all right. He said, "Yeah, why?" I responded, "Well, you don't seem too happy that I am on the computer. I am just doing some ministry work. I will be off in a minute. Are you sure you don't need anything?" He responded, "It's not that, but honey, you always seem to be doing something on the computer, and even more so on my days off." It hit me like a ton of bricks. He was right. I had grown accustomed to him being fine on the couch or doing his own thing. I had not taken time to be with him, much less include him in family needs.

As law enforcement wives we can get used to doing things on our own that we forget they need to be needed as well. Let's face it, as human beings, and as married couples, we need to feel needed in our home and in each other's lives. I got off the computer after wrapping up my work and then my mind began to wonder about what he said. What distractions were keeping me from pouring into my role in the home? If we are not careful we can steer away from fulfilling our purpose in the home. Many of our officers can do this too. Communication, along with including my officer in the home activities, reminds him that once he is rested, he needs join in and be with us. Not every household will struggle with this, but if we stay independent, we can shut them out unintentionally. Marriage is depending on the other, and that is a healthy thing! So, how are we to manage our time? This was something I prayed so long and hard about. I longed to know what that looked like for my family and I, but ultimately our household.

First and foremost, God will always be first. Here is

the thing, I see myself right next to God, walking with him, talking with him, and serving him with the strength he gives me. We cannot give what we don't have. Seeking God first allows me to see myself as God does. It allows me to love myself as he does and to be who he has called me to be. It can be easy to forget who we are, and when we do that we really have forgotten who God is. How? Because God is where our worth comes from, our purpose, and our identity. The time I spend praying is the time where I renew my strength, gain wisdom and understanding. I ask God to prepare me for what is to come.It reminds me of a plane trip. It is recommended that you place the oxygen mask on yourself before assisting others. We must be able to inhale before we exhale. Self-care is so vital and we will discuss that in the next chapter.

The second focus should be our husband. What? Not the kids next? No, the relationship with our husband is before that of our children. They were there before the children and will be there after they have gone. If we cannot display a healthy relationship, it can leave our children feeling unstable. Not everyone can set time for date nights, but it is important to have those intimate conversations and time alone. The both of you must pour into your marriage and nurture it. Our children will grow up, venture into the world, and you and your spouse will remain. That is not to say you can't reconnect after all those years, but imagine if you nurtured your marriage, how different it would be. Imagine what the next phase of your marriage would be like. A new season of adventure! The children are next! Our kids on duty are truly beside us as we walk this blue line. His call to duty is not just his. It is one badge, one purpose, and our family. I cannot stress that enough! While we cannot shield them from everything, we can certainly try. As we fight to keep peace in our homes, we equally fight to ensure our children have peace in their hearts. The idea of what their father truly does unfolds as they grow. Their father will always be a hero, there is never a doubt about that. In their young and innocent days they know him as the one who catches the bad guys or the one who gets to speed away with lights and sirens. However, as they grow, the depth of their understanding grows even deeper which can either cause fear, anxiety, or frustration.

Our children have faced one of those at some time or another. For our oldest he saw his father's call to duty as something almost glamorous. He wanted the play with toy handcuffs, a plastic Dollar Tree badge, and the nerf gun as he and his brother played cops and robbers. Fast forward to his teen years and out of nowhere he exclaimed how he "hates" that daddy is a police officer. With tear filled eyes he could only think of how hard this call to duty really is. He shared how much worry entered his thoughts. The possibility of losing his father became real, and a reality he wasn't ready to face. Does he truly understand the word "hate"? I doubt it. He hated the anxiety, worry, and fear that came along with the knowledge of what his father truly is called to. His heart is tender and his compassion is astounding. He has learned there are days he must pray against fear. He has also found himself deeply appreciating his father's arrival from the beat. Funny thing is he loves his friends to know his father is a cop. He beams when he mentions what his father does. But each child in our household and in yours will be different in their views.

Let me introduce you to our middle son, who is also a teenager. This fierce boy longs to follow in his father's footsteps. With all confidence and knowledge, he knows his father has to do it. Now this particular child is a miniature version of his father in every way. He is soft and tender, yet tough and bold. He says, "The job has to be done no matter how ugly it gets." How my mommy heart aches and worries for him as he grows into the man God has called him to be, which is possibly a future officer. I would love to shield him, but this call to duty cannot be ignored. If anything, we want to nurture that part of his desire to be in law enforcement. His father is always teaching him what he knows. If you put these two together around a patrol car, you will catch our son being observant, wanting to learn all its functions. He is the one who tells me not to get out of the car at the grocery store and asks if I know why. I always laugh and ask, "Ok, why?" He will tell me to be aware of my surroundings at all times! He has such an officer's heart.

Now, let me introduce you to our daughter, the princess. She is another tender heart in our home with a pinch of sass. She is the one who sees at a different level. She is a nurturer and showers her daddy with love and wisdom. There was a day when he was very exhausted, almost stressed, and she sat next to him on the bed. She put her little hands around him and said, "Just know that it's okay." She has such insight in understanding what this call to duty can do. She worries sometimes, but never allows it to consume her. If anything, she is an extension of God's heart when it comes to her father.

Perhaps I described one of your children as you read through each our children's personalities. Maybe I didn't. As I shared before, each child is unique. Seek out their weaknesses and strengths. Encourage them to thrive in those strengths as they live as a child of an officer. No matter what, each child will be different, and as parents we must pray about how we are to raise them to walk this thin blue line. We also want them to recognize that this is a part of our lives, not our lives completely.

What I have found to be true is that they will respond how we respond. My father always told me, "Watch how you respond, they are watching. How you respond, they will too." That stuck with me as a police wife and parent. What my father said has truly been wisdom I turn to with each passing circumstance we face as a family.

There is a local police wife who has taught me so much when it comes to responding in this life. When there is a fallen officer, you can always count on her making the news. She and her children make a precious statement in the local newspaper. She never speaks to the media, but her actions speak a thousand words in utter silence. She takes her children by the hand and lays flowers, balloons, along with handmade posters filled with crayon and pictures. As I witnessed her actions, I thought, "This woman is teaching her kids to honor." They may be younger than six years of age, but she is already laying the foundation for them. She is showing them what it looks like to walk the line. All I know is when we watch her do this, it is her actions that speak louder than any words she could ever speak.

It is my goal to ensure my children do not allow this life to consume them or cause fear. If anything, I tell them they must believe in something bigger than themselves, and that is God. Prayer has been the foundation in their life as they navigate being a kid on duty. Our ultimate goal in our heavenly substations should be keeping God at the center. When we do this, it allows God to reach the unreachable places in our family's hearts, minds, and souls.

Just when you think your husband and children are the only ones who need you, we find that work or ministry requires our time too. Some of you work inside the home and some work outside the home. But no matter what, as a wife on duty, you truly set the heart of the home.

Now, can we talk about beat dust?

Beat dust, you are probably wondering what that is. I use this term because our officer's patrol the beat and go into dark places where they are not wanted. Somehow or in some way, they will experience rejection at any call. For example, the battered wife calls for help, yet screams in anger when she feels the police are hurting her husband. The random drug bust where everyone scatters to get away from them. Sadly, the spit in the burger they ordered for lunch while in uniform, or the slammed door in their face as they are refused service.

The badge they bear brings rejection, hatred, controversy, and division. Why? Because they are the line between good and evil. As they enter those places, all of it falls on them. It falls on them like dust. Even Jesus knew we would experience rejection when it came to spreading the good news and doing his work. God gave us instruction about what to do before entering our home or any place we were not welcome.

> *And if anyone will not receive you or listen*
> *to your words, shake off the dust from*
> *your feet when you leave that house*
> *or town.*
>
> — MATTHEW 10:14 ESV

This idea of shaking the dust off one's feet is a symbolic meaning. This meaning is the same as understanding and acknowledging that one has done all that can be done in a situation they face. In understanding that, it allows the person to leave it in God's hands and know there is no further responsibility for it. Such examples are written in the word of God where Jesus sends his disciples out to preach the gospel to everyone. When the disciples were received with joy, he asked that they stay and teach. But if they were rejected, they had no further responsibility and could walk away. This allowed for a clear conscience as they knew there was nothing more they could do. Shaking the dust off their feet made a statement. It was like saying,

"You may have rejected me, but you can't cling to me or stop me from what I was called to do."

There are situations our officer's face, ourselves included, where God calls us to stand firm or to move forward. As we "shake the dust off our feet" we surrender those people or situations to God and allow ourselves to emotionally or mentally let go. Our officers are called to where they are dispatched. In that, they are responsible for bringing order to chaos. However, where they are not received, they must understand they did all they could. Should they be rejected, spat upon, or death spoken over them, they are ultimately not responsible for the outcome or the lives of those they served.

The focus of dusting off their feet is that they realize those they encounter are to be left in God's hands. By the mental, emotional, and spiritual process of dusting off their feet, they will learn to not bring it home. The beat dust could be scattered all over your home even now. There could be depression over the baby they saw dead, anger from the old man who was beaten, rage from the idea and belief that they didn't do enough, or sadness from the death notification given.

There are times we must shake the dust off our feet. This will lead to a clear conscience, sound mind, and a full trust. When we have those three things, we understand that we did everything we could to reach those God sent to us, and who God dispatched our officers to. We are to serve no matter the outcome because that is out of our control.

Our homes are more than just structure, it is built up to what we create it to be. What we bring in daily can change the atmosphere. As wives we are not exempt. We too will face rejection and we will equally need to dust off our feet.

One other door that is important in your home is that of your bedroom. As a couple you sleep there, rest, dress, and intimacy takes place. There is that word again, intimacy. But in the bedroom intimacy can mean deep conversations and yes, sex.

This act of love was given by God as a gift. Perhaps the ultimate wedding gift. For years we struggled in the bedroom. How many of you are struggling even now? So many factors can be a detriment in our sex life. It could be stress, health concerns, lack of energy, lack of time, medication, or in my case, molestation from my childhood.

It was the toughest battle I faced as a child. When I was in second grade, my teacher was pregnant, and we knew she would be out for a long while as she took maternity leave. As any child would be, we were all excited to have a substitute – someone different from our teacher. The arrival of my teacher's baby came, and we had a male substitute who was also a pastor. We students had thought the time with a substitute teacher would be exciting and fun, but it was not. After a few weeks of having our substitute, he began to touch me in inappropriate ways. I was being molested, and at the time, I had no idea how to find safety or expose his behavior. I didn't understand what was happening to me. All I knew was I felt uncomfortable, sick, scared, and so alone.

I recall many times I would look across at the principal's office and wondered if I should just run and scream. But each time I stayed quiet and stood still; I was unable to move. A few more weeks passed. I was at gymnastics, and I remember seeing my mother come in with tears in her eyes. She grabbed me and took me outside, apologizing for not knowing. The substitute teacher also had molested my best friend, and the police were at her house, taking a report. I remember thinking it was finally over. It was now out in the open, and I could finally breathe.

Each time I looked back it brought anger and pain. Maybe it was then I realized I was in a pit. All those years I may have physically left that classroom, but deep down I was still there frozen in fear. I had bitterness toward men and thought of them as dirty and selfish for their own sexual desires. My parents preferred not to tell family or friends what happened, as molestation was not spoken of back then. Counseling? Never got it. It was to be brushed under the rug and so I lived my life leaving it in the past. I have never blamed my parents. I understood it was easier to leave it behind, than to face it head on. The process was too painful to deal with, not just for me, but my parents as well.

Because intimacy is a part of marriage, this brought conflict. I knew I needed healing so I could stop being quiet, as I had done as a little girl. Healing needed to come and the process needed to happen. I prayed for God to help me, He was the only one who could. This was definitely an area in my marriage where God could take all the enemy meant for harm, and turn it into a place of restoration. Intimacy, sex, is a gift given by God to enjoy and take pleasure in with our spouse. I found myself struggling in this and my husband's touch was something I had to have control over. I viewed sex as a bad and dirty thing not to be discussed.

Each time my husband reached out for me, I would brush him off or even walk away to avoid it. I recall a time that my husband came up behind me in the kitchen to give me a kiss and be flirtatious. I told him, "Honey, we just got back from church." He looked surprised and confused, and said, "But you're my wife." In that moment I realized touch was still dirty to me. My mentality was that of a little girl fighting to feel free of unwanted touch.

Our husband's touch and desire to be with us

should be viewed as a blessing. We should want them to touch us. It should not be viewed as disgusting, annoying, or a problem. Unfortunately, many can be robbed of the gift of intimacy when sexual assault, molestation, or any form of sexual hurt has occurred. All these years I have felt as if I was given a broken gift. It was as if someone came along, took my perfect gift, broke it, and returned it back to me. This marital gift of intimacy had been distorted in my life.

Before this book revision occurred, I mentioned praying for the man who molested me. So much more has happened since, and I am excited to share it with you.

A few years back, I began searching his name in the sex offender database. At first I wasn't sure why. When his photo popped up, a flood of emotions came over me. I wanted to pray for him as I knew it was the right thing to do, but anger was far greater in me than forgiveness. I sat for months visiting his profile until one day I was ready to utter some life changing words.

"Lord, help me forgive him. I want to be free".

Talk about a daring request. I would pray for him with so much resistance.

As time went by, a random moment occurred that made my journey to forgive accelerate. I was folding

laundry while my boys were watching, "Karate Kid
II" and from the other room I heard Mr. Miyagi
speak words that pierced my heart. Yes, I know it
sounds silly, but it threw me for a loop! He had just
finished defending one of the Cobra Kai students
from their abusive instructor. Daniel realized Mr.
Miyagi could have killed him with one blow and
when he mentioned it, wisdom came out. Mr.
Miyagi in his awesome broken accent said,
"Because, Daniel san – for person with no
forgiveness in heart. Living even worse punishment
than death." BOOM! That shook me to the core not
only for myself, but for the man who molested
me too.

My immediate thought was, "Could he be living in
condemnation? Has he forgiven himself for such
horrific actions?" That thought broke my heart. Why
out of nowhere was I feeling compassion for a man
who deserves no forgiveness?

I took my boys to a soccer field so I could walk while
they played. I began to pray until my prayer turned
into a conversation with this man who hurt me. It
dawned on me, I need to write him a letter. I wasn't
sure when it would happen, but I knew when it was
time. I also knew God would show me how and tell
me when. A month passed and I woke up one
morning with an urgency to write. This urgency was
so strong I told my children to wait for breakfast
and sat down with a paper and pen. The words

flowed from my fingers and before I knew it, I concluded in black ink,

"From someone who forgives you"

There it was, a letter written with words of forgiveness. But now what? Later that day I visited his sex offender profile. I scrolled through it and his address appeared. My heart sank at the thought of mailing it. I grabbed the letter, put it in an envelope, and mailed it off. Placing the letter in the mailbox was like putting broken chains that fell off my heart. I felt freedom again. It was an emotional time. To this day I don't know if he received it or who read it. What I do know is, it is well with my soul.

Since that day I have not looked at his photo. It has been years. But from time to time, his name is spoken on my lips as I pray for him. Forgiving him does not excuse his behavior. I know he didn't deserve it. But I can't help and think of what the cross truly means. It means God has it covered, not just for me, but for all of us.

Intimacy. It is a too valuable to not fight for. At the beginning of our marriage I had not shared my childhood experience with my husband. I continued to hide it, till it was no longer able to be hidden. If you have been affected by sexual abuse, please communicate with your spouse. I never realized how much I kept my husband in the dark about my struggle. He became a huge part of the healing process with his understanding, patience, and grace. As I shared my experience with him, it allowed him to better understand my feelings and reason behind my resistance. He walked the journey with me and still does.

Lack of desire toward intimacy is not always based on sexual abuse. As I mentioned before, there are many factors that affect our sex drive. If you are struggling in this area, please consult a physician so you and your husband can enjoy a healthy sex life. Coming together as husband and wife is vital. Remember what brought you two together – love. From that love you started a family, and ultimately created a home. Each home will be so unique. As you create your home environment, remember to guard it from the world and all its chaos. Although we discussed specific parts of the house, the entire household is precious. It is a place where you can be your own "family".

REFLECTION

- Have you thought about your front door and what truly happens there? What are your thoughts?
- Are there distractions that keep you from being the wife or mother your household needs? Draw a picture of a plate and then write out all your obligations on it, and see

how full your plate is. Then pray about what
needs to be removed.

- Being the wife of a first responder we tend
  to do things alone. Have you ever
  unintentionally excluded your husband from
  any activities?
- Is your heavenly substation a place of peace
  and rest? If not, what steps can you take to
  get there?
- One family, one call, one purpose was
  mentioned. What is your view toward your
  children in this life as a first responder
  family?
- As wives most of us have experienced the
  effects of the beat. We have witnessed anger,
  depression, seclusion, or silence from our
  first responder. Some of us have equally
  experienced these ourselves with daily
  stress. How does your household deal with
  beat dust and stress?

Father,

I thank you for the household and family you have
blessed me with. I come to you seeking wisdom and
how better to watch the things of my household.
Help me recognize anything that may harm my
children, myself, or our marriage. As I live my life,

help me to manage my time and make it pleasing to you.

I ask that you reveal any distractions that keep our family from quality time together. Help our household to know that we can say "no" to others in a healthy way and set our priorities so that others will know of our responsibilities.

I thank you, Lord, for helping us as we journey through this life and for watching over our household when we can't. I pray our home will be Christ-centered and that my husband and children will seek you. Help my husband lead our family with your grace and love. I pray that even with the busyness of life, our home will be a home of order and rest. May we be reminded that our home is more than a physical structure, it is a place of intimacy.

In Jesus name, Amen

TRUTH

The wise woman builds her house, but with her own hands the foolish one tears hers down.

— PROVERBS 14:1 NIV

For every house is built by someone, but God is the builder of everything.

— HEBREWS 3:4 NIV

My people will live in peaceful dwelling places, in secure homes, in undisturbed places of rest.

— ISAIAH 32:18 NIV

But if serving the Lord seems undesirable to you, then choose for yourselves this day whom you will serve, whether the gods your ancestors served beyond the Euphrates, or the gods of the Amorites, in whose land you are living. But as for me and my household, we will serve the Lord.

— JOSHUA 24:15 NIV

The rain came down, the streams rose, and the winds blew and beat against that house; yet it did not fall, because it had its foundation on the rock.

— MATTHEW 7:25 NIV

AND ON THE SEVENTH DAY

I am sure many of you completed the title of this chapter with, "He rested." That's because in the scriptures after God created the heavens and the earth, he rested! You can now smile from ear to ear because this chapter is about YOU resting!

Rest is important and many of us don't appreciate the value of it. As wives on duty, we become consumed with providing care for everyone, but ourselves. We have attended numerous sports games, recitals, award ceremonies, or holiday events alone. Without realizing, we grow accustomed to the load we carry. By doing this, it can be too much to bear if we are not careful. As your officer goes above and beyond for his family and city, you go above and beyond for him and your family.

As we walk the thin blue line, rest will be your best friend, your sanity, and strength. It will take being intentional and putting into practice what the Lord has called us to do.

> Remember the Sabbath day by keeping it
> holy. Six days you shall labor and do all
> your work, but the seventh day is a
> Sabbath to the Lord your God. On it you
> shall not do any work, neither you, nor
> your son or daughter, nor your male or
> female servant, nor your animals, nor
> any foreigner residing in your towns.

— EXODUS 20:8-10 NIV

You see, even the Lord requires us to rest, to the point he considers it holy. He knew we would need time to pull away and be still. Have you ever heard the phrase, "You can't pour out on an empty cup?" Well, it's true! Self-care is so important. How can you give what you don't have? Before you start rolling your eyes and think, "Yeah right, that is not going to happen", please consider the effects of not making rest a priority.

There was a day I received a text message asking for my officer's assistance. His days off had been minimal to none that week, and I knew not having boundaries was unwise. I also knew he needed rest, a break, and I wanted to protect that. I was defensive when it came to his time off, especially his rest. I debated on whether I should tell my husband about the person in need or respond to the text alerting this person that he was resting. I admit it, my flesh got the best of me and I told them he was resting, but that he would get back to them soon.

The problem back then was, saying "no" was not easy for me personally. It became harder for me when I saw others were in need. When others didn't volunteer, I was the first to commit myself despite knowing I had no time in the day to complete it. But somehow, I managed. I became better at saying no to protect my husband and his rest, but never learned to say no for myself. I never thought about myself or even cared that I was wearing myself out. I spoke frequently about never getting any rest. I made it known to the world that I was sacrificing and bearing my cross. I ensured my officer knew that I never got a break. After all, I was tough, I could handle anything that came my way. As my dad would jokingly say, "I am woman, hear me roar." This independent heart of mine leaned on her own understanding. My to-do list was going to get done one way or the other. At night while everyone slept, I kept going. I was the first to wake up and the last to go to sleep. I clearly didn't trust the Lord. I say that with a heavy heart because back then I had to have control.

No matter how much I did or didn't do, each day came with more expectations and its demands piled up. The thing is, my to-do list piled so high at times I couldn't see ahead. Going to sleep each night was something I looked forward to each day, yet the minute I hit the pillow, my mind wouldn't shut off. I was restless and lacked sleep. Although I was lying in bed, I was still not resting because I was focused on the million things I needed to get done. I was trying to figure out who, what, where, when, and why! My prayers were no more than a few minutes and a part of the to-do list. In fact, prayer is what I should have done all along, but not out of obligation, only out of desire.

Now let's fast forward to a day where I was exhausted from all of life's expectations. It was a day I chose to stay in pajamas and do absolutely nothing. Truth is I had nothing in me to give. Normally, I would have been all over the place. I was always in and outside of the house because I didn't know how to simply rest.

My body, mind, and emotions were run down to nothing. I sat on the couch with a blanket wrapped around me. Dark circles were evident under my eyes and my unwashed hair was placed in a messy bun. My phone would go off and I ignored it. My husband said it perfectly that day, "Honey, you are not yourself."

Suddenly, the doorbell rang. My husband and I stared at each other. I was so exhausted I didn't say a word. My husband looked at me and said, "Go upstairs. I will handle it." I went upstairs and sat at the top step with my head leaning against the wall.

I could hear conversing, my husband and a woman sharing laughter, and then the door slammed. Pure silence. My husband went up to get me and tell me the coast was clear! Turned out this sweet lady we know was treating us to a pie. I went back downstairs to join him on the couch. I hugged him and began to cry. I was in no position to be around others. I was flat out depleted. I had fought to protect my officer's rest, but never fought to protect mine.

As I put my head on his chest I felt safe, as if I was in his arms hiding from the world. I should have never allowed myself to reach such a place of exhaustion. I never did it on purpose. My intentions of "doing it all" was never to run myself down. I felt that if I wasn't always doing something, then I was doing nothing.

But what truly happened is, I forgot my hiding place was not to be in the arms of my husband, but in the arms of Jesus. Sure, my husband's arms are amazing, I love being there. However, only God could reach the depths of my heart and places my husband cannot reach. Only God could renew my strength, give me peace, and refresh my soul.

> For you are my hiding place; you protect me
> from trouble. You surround me with
> songs of victory.

— PSALM 32:7 NLT

Over the years I have learned to become more dependent on God and seek him when I need rest. Don't get me wrong, there are times when I forget and get caught up in the hustle and bustle, but I have equally learned to be more intentional. I have found that asking for help is not being weak, it is being strong. I also learned that my husband can protect my time to rest as well. It is all about communicating to those around us when we need rest and ensuring we make time to do it.

There is a story in the bible about two sisters, Mary and Martha. These two ladies were about to have Jesus come to their house. Now, one of them felt the need to labor despite Jesus being in her home, while the other decided she would rest at the feet of Jesus. Seriously, if I knew Jesus was coming over to my house, you know I would have been scrubbing and polishing like crazy.

I probably would have been in the kitchen preparing my infamous Spaghetti Casserole and sweet Texas tea. Having Jesus over was a pretty big deal. So in Martha's defense, she was hosting this gathering and we can't blame her for wanting everything to be perfect. Now Miss Mary on the other hand just wanted to sit at the feet of Jesus and take him all in. She was absorbing the moment with Jesus. As sisters do, they bicker. Martha got upset and made sure Jesus knew that her sister Mary was not helping her at all! Check it out......

> *As Jesus and his disciples were on their way,*
> *he came to a village where a woman*
> *named Martha opened her home to him.*
> *She had a sister called Mary, who sat at*
> *the Lord's feet listening to what he said.*
> *But Martha was distracted by all the*
> *preparations that had to be made. She*
> *came to him and asked, "Lord, don't you*
> *care that my sister has left me to do the*
> *work by myself? Tell her to help me!"*
>
> — LUKE 10:38-40 NIV

So much was happening that day. Martha was hosting, Mary was basically a guest too, yet we all know deep down Martha wanted to finish all the preparation so she too could sit and enjoy Jesus. Yet, she got frustrated. She probably felt like so many of us do each day enslaved in our to-do list that we become frustrated. Of course we want to rest, of course we want to stop, but we feel as if we can't because then nothing will get done. But Jesus said something profound to Martha.

> *"Martha, Martha," the Lord answered, "You are worried and upset about many things, but few things are needed—or indeed only one. Mary has chosen what is better, and it will not be taken away from her."*
>
> — LUKE 10:38-40 NIV

I read that and I was like, "Really Jesus? The poor girl was trying to make it special." But if we look at this story, how many of us are Martha's in this wife on duty life? How many of us are worried and upset about so many things when few things are needed? Can you imagine if you were to stop and just sit at the feet of Jesus? When we choose the better as Mary did, then we find rest.

When we choose to sit at his feet, it is then we can hear his voice and know what needs to be done. Seeking God first is a total game changer. While Martha was so busy "trying" to make everything special, the moment Jesus arrived made it all special. No matter what she did that day, the point was missed with her to-do list.

"But seek first his kingdom and his righteousness, and all these things will be given to you as well. Therefore do not worry about tomorrow, for tomorrow will worry about itself. Each day has enough trouble of its own."

— MATTHEW 6:33-34 NLV

Each day really does have trouble of its own. All the nights we stay up worrying or trying to devise a plan to accomplish everything at once, will get us nowhere unless we sit at the feet of Jesus. Rest on purpose. Seeking God allows us to hand over the load in our lives and find the rest we all desperately need.

I have a planner filled with all sorts of colorful ink and stickers. To this day I fill it out and it keeps me focused on what needs to be done. However, I have disciplined myself to ensure that I have time to rest each day. Although my agenda is written in ink, I ensure to keep it mentally penciled in. I understand that if things don't get done, there is always another day.

No to mention I pray for the Lord's will to be done and not my own. This will mean interruptions, canceled events, or an executive decision to rest when I find my body or family need it.

Come to me, all you who are weary and
burdened, and I will give you rest. Take
my yoke upon you and learn from me, for
I am gentle and humble in heart, and you
will find rest for your souls. For my yoke
is easy and my burden is light."

— MATTHEW 11:28-30 NIV

All things flow from our heart. If we are constantly doing things, we will eventually lose joy. We will fall trap to routine and become irritated when things get in the way of our accomplishing them. We will do things out of obligation instead of love. As you can see, the first important step in rest is that of seeking God first. God created you and knows the depths of your heart. Only he can fulfill and give you what is needed to accomplish his will. Let God be your hiding place. Let him take the burden from your heart and lead your every step.

 God first. God created you and knows the depths of your heart.

Ask yourself if prayer is something you feel obligated to do or don't want to do. If so, ask God to help you desire to seek him more. A one minute prayer of bold faith is far greater than a ten minute prayer of empty words. When we pray, it should not be routine, it should be because we desire to sit at his feet. I can't tell you how many times I have chosen to sit at his feet while praying, despite having a million things to do. Yet, somehow everything that matters gets done and I find the Lord stretches my time.

There are so many ways to rest. Sometimes we need to get creative. Rest can be from five minutes to a full day, it all depends on what you need to be productive and to be the best possible you. Remember, it's okay to ask for help. You are loved and those around you will want to see you enjoy life without the hustle and bustle. Just like you schedule time for your to-do list, schedule time for your rest.

Protect the time you set aside to refresh yourself and ensure boundaries are set. If you have a hard time saying no there is an amazing book called, "The Best Yes", by Lysa Terkeurst. That book truly helped me when it came to not just doing things, but doing God's thing. After all, we want to be intentional women. We equally don't want to miss out on God's opportune moments to share with our families, to be a light in someone's day, and to simply have the blessing of sitting at the feet of Jesus.

Wives on duty, we may not always have it all together. We may not have answers or time to do it all. But we should know this, we are wives of officers and we are strong enough.

REFELECTION

- Do you take time to rest? If no, why not? If yes, what do you find rest does for your mind, body, and soul?
- Do you find yourself easily carried away in your to-do list? How can you cut back when it comes to lessening your load?
- In the story of Mary and Martha, who do you relate to most?
- Do you have a hard time saying no? If so, why do you think this is?
- What steps will you take to ensure you have time to rest?

Lord,

I thank you for the reminder to rest in our lives. Forgive me if I have chosen to go about my business instead of resting at your feet each day. Help me be intentional when it comes to caring for myself. Surround me with people willing to help when life becomes too much. Remind me that in you is where I find my hiding place and strength.

Renew my strength Lord and help me to be the best follower of Christ I can be. Give me wisdom when it's time to say no and wisdom when it's time to say yes. Lord, let me do your things, your will, and not my own. Let my every action be on purpose.

Amen

TRUTH

Do you not know? Have you not heard? The Lord is the everlasting God, the creator of all the earth. He never grows weak or weary. No one can measure the depths of his understanding. He gives power to the weak and strength to the powerless. Even youths will grow weak in exhaustion. But those who trust in the Lord will find new strength. They will soar high among wings like eagles; they will run and not grow weary, they will walk and not faint.

— ISAIAH 40:28-31 NIV

For you are my hiding place; you protect me from trouble. You surround me with songs of victory.

— PSALM 32:7 NIV

*In peace I will lie down and sleep. For you
alone, Lord, make me dwell in safety.*

— PSALM 4:8 NIV

*Come to me, all you who are weary and
burdened, and I will give you rest. Take
my yoke upon you and learn from me, for
I am gentle and humble in heart, and you
will find rest for your souls. For my yoke
is easy and my burden is light.*

— MATTHEW 11:28-30 NIV

*But seek first his kingdom and his
righteousness, and all these things will
be given to you as well. Therefore do not
worry about tomorrow, for tomorrow
will worry about itself. Each day has
enough trouble of its own.*

— MATTHEW 6:33-34 NLV

THE PURSUIT

In the line of duty, officers will end up in a pursuit at times. These pursuits are a chase to capture those who violated the law. However, the pursuit I speak of is seeking to have an unshakeable faith and an unshakeable marriage.

I remember years ago receiving an invitation to a woman's bible study. Back then I rolled my eyes at the thought. I wondered what good it would do. My marriage felt beyond repair and I was in no mood to listen to advice or opinions. Then, in all honesty I found out there would be food....hmmm....I guess I could go. So, I went. The room was full of laughter, hugs, and women that appeared to have it all together. You know, smiling and all dolled up without a care in the world. I grabbed my plate of food and made sure I sat in the back where no one would really notice me. And so it began, the topic: marriage.

The discussion and shared content was all about the "good" things in marriage. All the ladies mentioned kind gestures or the mushy love notes they left for their husbands. As for me, I was thinking, "Yeah, that ain't happening in my house." Everyone was all googly eyed over their husband and I was irritated with mine. I was about to tune them out and enjoy more food when a lady said, "The secret to love is to pour despite. To forgive despite. But mainly to not wait till something breaks in your marriage. It will require nurturing to thrive."

She had my attention. A light bulb went on in my head and it all made sense. Suddenly the broccoli and ranch on my plate didn't matter. I was now listening. All the mushy love notes they spoke of or how they went out of their way to love on their husband was not to be judged. If anything, they were being wise. They didn't have it all together, that's why they were all there, myself included. Why did I think I never needed to nurture our marriage unless it was failing? All the invitations I turned down, all the marriage counsel I chose not to listen to, or the retreats I felt we didn't need because nothing was wrong.

Point is, don't wait till it's broken. When things are great we forget to nurture. We can easily take marriage for granted. The mundane can take over and we grow accustomed to just "being" there in our daily routine. I thought about all the missed opportunities in my marriage. There were moments we were invited to marriage retreats only to decline since we felt it was only for troubled marriages. The advice our parents gave us were things that went in one ear and out the other. I remember choosing a girls night instead of a date night with my husband. But when we reached a breaking point, then I was willing to do what was needed. I was willing to do what I should have done all along.

I say this with love to you precious wife on duty, don't wait till it's broken. Marriage takes nurturing, giving, and pursuing the desired goal of a healthy marriage. Marriage can be unpredictable, therefore be ready and willing to do all needed in good times and in bad. And learn from my young self, accept the invitations once in a while. You never know what you will learn.

Also, don't wait to seek God till it's broken. Pursue God in the good and bad times. Pray diligently for your marriage and husband. Surround yourself with women and others who want to see your marriage succeed and thrive.

When I think of the pursuit in our lives to follow God's design for our marriage, I think of the story of

Peter. We can find this story of pursuit in the book of Matthew.

"Immediately Jesus made the disciples get into the boat and go on ahead of him to the other side, while he dismissed the crowd. After he had dismissed them, he went up on a mountainside by himself to pray. Later that night, he was there alone, and the boat was already a considerable distance from land, buffeted by the waves because the wind was against it. Shortly before dawn Jesus went out to them, walking on the lake. When the disciples saw him walking on the lake, they were terrified. "It's a ghost," they said, and cried out in fear.

But Jesus immediately said to them: "Take courage! It is I. Don't be afraid."

> *"Lord, if it's you," Peter replied, "tell me to come to you on the water." "Come," he said. Then Peter got down out of the boat, walked on the water and came toward Jesus. But when he saw the wind, he was afraid and, beginning to sink, cried out, "Lord, save me!" Immediately Jesus reached out his hand and caught him. "You of little faith," he said, "why did you doubt?" And when they climbed into the boat, the wind died down."*

> — MATTHEW 14:22-32 NIV

How often do we experience Peter moments? These are moments we find ourselves bold in the Lord, ready to respond to his call, and daring to believe the impossible. Then, the winds of life blow around us, and we take notice of it. Our focus then turns to the circumstances or trials, instead of Jesus. Just like Peter, at times we dare step out of the boat, and once something doesn't look right, we panic. However, I love that Peter knew the son of man would reach down and save him. Jesus simply told him to, "come". He never said to come and be cautious, he simply called his child and expected Peter to keep his eyes focused on his.

We must remember that this life will bring trial. Yet we hold a promise in James 1:2-4 NIV that says,

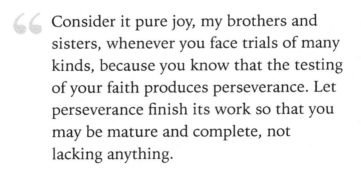

Consider it pure joy, my brothers and sisters, whenever you face trials of many kinds, because you know that the testing of your faith produces perseverance. Let perseverance finish its work so that you may be mature and complete, not lacking anything.

This is why your pursuit to obtain an unshakeable faith and marriage will be effective. It will turn you into a woman of perseverance, mature, complete, and lacking nothing. As you pursue the Lord in this life, you will find that even if life circumstances try to shake you, you will be rooted into the strong rock of Jesus Christ.

So, I leave you with this. I remember one night, my officer and I were watching a television show and laughed at all the same parts. I held his hand gently and could only imagine what those sweet hands did earlier in the day. I knew he cuffed someone and shook hands as he met an elderly man seeking a conversation. With all he shared about his day on the beat, I knew there was more and could only wonder about the rest of his day. The hands of a first responder have many stories to tell. Some of bravery, panic, heroic, yet gut wrenching. Their hands can be worn from the beat. Perhaps you have found cuts, scrapes, bruising, or a broken finger from the scuffles or pursuits. Their hands speak volumes.

And then there are the hands of a wife on duty, your hands. These hands equally have stories to tell. As stated before, these hands wipe tears, rinse off blood from uniforms, hold the faces of a broken first responder, hold the hand of their officer to assure support, and hands that need no words because they were created to help. The help of a wife on duty's hands is far from understood. It is a secret place with stories that often go unnoticed, some unnoticed by a wife on duty herself. Her hands often don't get credit. When was the last time you stopped and realized the importance of your role?

The hands of a wife on duty have a strength to do what many couldn't, they have an equal amount of tenderness and boldness, and they are the definition of support.

Wives on duty, know that the work of your hands are appreciated. None of what you do is in vain. Each of you come from all walks of life, yet it doesn't change the fact that you are precious in the eyes of God. He wants you to pursue him. Your pursuit in faith and in marriage will be a huge part of your testimony. Your pursuit for greater things will be your legacy. Your pursuit in this wife on duty life will be your story. So, what will it be?

Remember, being a wife on duty is a journey and unfolding story. It's full of every kind of emotion you can think of. At times patience, strength, and courage is put to the test. There are times when you feel stuck, like there is nothing more to give. There are days where you wonder if you are second and tired of it. There are days where it is straight up hard, yet you do it. For one, you sacrifice, and not a little, a lot!

Second, you give! You give your time, shared protection, give up, give in, and give till you run out sometimes. But you do it. You pour so much while nothing is being poured in and depletion takes over. But you do it. So many may ask how you do it, and you can say, "It is God in me who does it." Don't be hard on yourself, allow yourself "those days" and throw your hands in the air and simply say, "Jesus". If we keep it real here, we will quickly see no-one has it all together, not a single one of us is perfect. As wives on duty let us thrive, not just survive. So yeah, you are a big deal, a vital part of the thin blue line, and precious to God. Your story is yours and the outcome is still to come. But in every circumstance, never stop pursuing. Never stop being who God created you to be.

REFLECTION

- What does the word "pursuit" mean to you when it comes to faith? Marriage?
- Have you found yourself in a Peter type moment? If so, what was the situation and the outcome?
- Have you ever felt no need to seek out marriage resources, or ways to stay healthy in marriage simply because there was nothing broken?
- Do you find that you decline or than accept invitations to retreats, conferences, or bible studies?
- What will do to pursue a strong and unshakable faith and marriage?

Lord,

I thank you for the grace you extend even in my times of doubt. Help me keep my eyes focused on you when the storms of life come. Guide me in this life and as I journey as a wife on duty. Lead me into a strong prayer life. Surround me with people who will sharpen me as I pursue more of you. Help my husband and I to be proactive in our marriage, never stagnant, and intentional when it comes to fulfilling our vows. Bring amazing godly resources our way and a community of people who will guide us in our marriage. We praise you for your faithfulness, even when we are not.

Amen

TRUTH

Let love and faithfulness never leave you;
bind them around your neck, write them
on the tablet of your heart. Then you will
win favor and a good name in the sight
of God and man.

— PROVERBS 3:3-4 NIV

And now these three remain: faith, hope and
love. But the greatest of these is love.

— 1 CORINTHIANS 13:13 NIV

*Let the morning bring me word of your
unfailing love, for I have put my trust in
you. Show me the way I should go, for to
you I entrust my life.*

— PSALM 143:8 NIV

*So do not fear, for I am with you; do not be
dismayed for I am your God. I will
strengthen you and help you; I will
uphold you with my righteous hand.*

— ISAIAH 41:10 NIV

*But the Lord stood at my side and gave me
strength, so that through me the message
might be fully proclaimed and all the
Gentiles might hear it. And I was
delivered from the lion's mouth.*

— 2 TIMOTHY 4:17 NIV

AFTERWORD

Now that you have completed this book, I am sure you see the importance and power of our stories. I know my story is one of millions out there. So now, it is a privilege to introduce you to a wife on duty named Jessica. This is her story...

My love and I have been married for over twenty years! We have two amazing adult children! My hero has twenty plus years in the military and police department including the SWAT team. Our marriage started off with a bang! We only knew each other less than a year before we were married. We grew up in two totally different worlds. We both brought our share of baggage to the marriage. We have experienced our share of hard times, including several yearlong deployments, health scares, a brain tumor, financial troubles, and the normal marital

issues every marriage deals with. Then there was
the fear, infidelity, anger, and alcohol abuse, lack of
forgiveness, bitterness, PTSD, distrust, deception,
no communication, anxiety, and suicidal thoughts.
On the outside it looked amazing, but we were
falling apart.

Several years ago it all came out! Every last hurtful,
heart wrenching secret. We both cried and talked for
hours. I knew in my heart I didn't want to lose him.
The thought of losing him hurt more than the
secrets we were both revealing to each other.
 Divorce for me was not an option no matter what. I
know that now a days that sounds "old school".
After talking we decided to get help. We started
individual and couples counseling. Things seemed
to be getting better. We even started praying
together every morning. We were both growing in
our relationship with the Lord and with each other,
however there were strongholds that we still held
on to.

Two years later we were still struggling, going round
and round with the same issues. It was a spiritual
battle! Full on WAR! One evening while at our small
church group, the Lord began to show some things
to this couple that was there. Secrets that I only
knew. Secrets that my love only knew. The couple,
along with our group prayed with us. Chains were
broken! Strongholds were broken! All the bitterness,
anger and lack of forgiveness gone! All lies and

secrets gone! THANK YOU JESUS! For the longest time I had actual chest/heart pains. When we prayed and released the strongholds, immediately my pains went away! We both felt a freedom that we had never felt. God was so good that even the next day our sweet mentor sent us a sermon on "How to live a life of freedom in the Holy Spirit"! There is healing and restoration! We are a perfect example of that!

We are still learning to live that life of freedom in the Holy Spirit and we are still learning God's love for us. We have to know His love for us so that we can love our spouses the way we are supposed to! My husband and I are still praying together every morning, but the prayers have changed! The look out of our eyes is different, even to others! We are both aware of the daily battle, but now we are doing it together. I'm so excited to see where God is going to take us! I have a marriage now that is better than when we first got married! We are falling in love more and more every day! I love watching my righteous, Godly husband become the man/husband God created him to be! I love seeing the changes in myself to become the woman/wife God has created me to be!

So amazing to watch God come alive in both of us!

Our husbands are surrounded by evil every day and if we are not careful we can allow ourselves to let

the enemy lie to us. Cover yourself and your
husband and children daily with prayer. Cover them
with the whole armor of God! Speak the Word of
God over them and yourself! Fight for your husband
and your marriage! My love battles the criminals
and I battle with him in the spirit and together we
stand strong on the Word of God and His promises
to us! – Jessica

THE STAINING OF THE BRIDE

By: Allison P. Uribe

A spotless bride approached her officer to be. They vowed, promised, and took an oath. For better or worse, promising to thrive in what they couldn't foresee.

The first few months were not so hard, but something happened when he entered his patrol car. The screams, the yells, dead bodies he would view, this changed his heart and his bride clearly knew.

He would snap, grow silent, and create this distance. His bride would cry feeling so much resistance. She remembered the day she vowed to be there. For better or worse, this responsibility was in her care.

So helpless she cried as she remembered the day,

her white dress flowed freely and his heart was okay. There was a badge over his heart almost creating a wall, not many would understand the extremity of his call.

With each passing shift his bride hoped with such passion, that when he came home he wouldn't have a lot of distraction. She showed him compassion to understand and assure him with care, because the heart break he saw, reminded her that he felt God was not there.

Her wedding dress once white with such purity, was now stained from all this beat hostility. Who knew the oaths taken were so different indeed. An oath for her and an oath for his city.

Two oaths, one man, one more important than the other. The officer didn't see his bride was the one he should cover. With all the sadness, hurt, and pain she would see, this brought stains to her dress, to this wife on duty.

This marriage is unique so many still say, so she prays to the Lord to consume her every day. Then Jesus comes to hold her tight, for her dress in His presence would go from stained to white. It was then she felt peace and the Lord would say, "Sweet wife on duty, just know I am the way".

She surrendered it all, her officer and marriage. The Lord was pleased and led them into his presence. It was there that they thrived and their soiled hearts came alive. This life will bring stains from all heartache and calls, but with Jesus by your side, he will be Lord of all.

When this call to duty becomes tough for both officer and bride, just remember the wise still seek him and make Him their guide. No dispatcher or navigation could lead like Him, for the Lord establishes steps for those who seek Him.

So if you are a bride, a wife on duty with stains, call the name of Jesus and let him cleanse you today. You were not meant to live surviving each day, you were meant to thrive no matter what life brings your way. Your dress can be white with His precious blood. For the Lord says finding a wife is very, very good.

ABOUT THE AUTHOR

Allison P. Uribe is the founder of Wives on Duty
Ministries and author of Cuffs and Coffee - A
devotional for wives of America's law enforcement.
She is an ordained minister who also served as a
chaplain for the San Antonio Police
Department. Allison is a national conference
speaker and one of the directors for Bless
the Badge.

Made in the USA
Middletown, DE
14 February 2021